# Interesting Exposures of Administration

# Interesting Exposures of Administration

**Mahesh Chandra Dewedy**

**Ocean Books Pvt. Ltd.**
**ISO 9001:2015 Publishers**

*Published by*
**Ocean Books (P) Ltd.**
4/19 Asaf Ali Road,
New Delhi-110 002 (INDIA)
e-mail: info@oceanbooks.in

ISBN 978-81-8430-358-2
**INTERESTING EXPOSURES OF ADMINISTRATION**
*by* Mahesh Chandra Dewedy

*Edition*
2025

*Price*
₹ 300.00 (Rupees Three Hundred only)



*Printed at*
Narula Printers, Delhi

*This book is dedicated to the Victims of Administrative Hard-headedness, Prejudice, Haughtiness, Dishonesty and, above all, Hypocrisy*

# The Motivation

I am indebted to all the hypocrites who happened to come across my life as an I.P.S. Officer – and they were not in small numbers. In fact, credit goes exclusively to them for motivating me to write this book – albeit, post-retirement. Since I had to remain thick and thin with them during 38 years and 21 days of my administrative career, I could not escape knowing them intimately, feeling them closely and becoming one with them occasionally.

Hypocrisy presupposes existence of a fair degree of intelligence. A dunce cannot be a hypocrite and a hypocrite cannot be a dunce. No lizard or hawk would ever profess that stalking other animals stealthily with intent to kill them is a sin, but cunning human beings often profess honesty and saintliness as a cover for their dishonesty and wickedness. Although it is neither true nor fair to state that all intelligent people are hypocrites, yet empirically a direct correlation can be established between the dexterity of hypocrites and the degree of their intelligence.

The bureaucrats, having been selected through open competition, are – saving the 'honorable' exceptions – more intelligent, and therefore, many of them indulge in greater hypocrisies than the common man does. And the politicians, who become *Netas* only after proving their superior intelligence in leading the herd, take the pride of the place among the most dexterous hypocrites.

An interesting development is being noticed recently. As the 21st century is advancing, the dishonest and dishonorable acts are being reinterpreted to preclude most of them from the ambit of dishonesty. Earlier, irregular gain of any kind beyond worth ₹ 50 by *Babus* (government servants) or *Netas* (ministers, legislators, etc.) was considered dishonest, but now receiving lakhs in parliamentary voting by legislators (cash for voting Sibu Soren case) or becoming a *crorepati* in no time on the pretext of receiving '*premopahars*' from 'loving subjects' (Bahenji's Income-tax case) have been declared lawful. Limits of honesty are being so stretched that dishonesty can be pursued without pinching one's conscience 'unnecessarily'. What is more distressing is the fact that unlike their predecessors of the bygone days, the rulers of today are now taking lead in establishing new norms and their 'most obedient servants' (the bureaucrats) are religiously following their footsteps. Further, the animal kingdom's culture of big fish swallowing the small fish is being adopted by the powerful without any wrinkle on their conscience. In fact, even hypocritical pretensions are gradually becoming unnecessary for pursuing dishonourable acts.

I am penning down a few instances of my administrative career which expose the haughtiness, hard-headedness, and hypocrisy in administration. I hope that the readers will find them invariably revealing, often interesting, occasionally funny, and sometimes even hilarious.

**—Mahesh Chandra Dewedy**
'Gyan Prasar Sansthan'
1/137, Vivekkhand, Gomtinagar
Lucknow-226010
Phone-9415063030

# Contents


*The Motivation* 7

1. Choose Your Time and Place 11
2. *Aap To Na Jaane Kaise I.P.S. Me Aa Gaye!* 15
3. Out of Sync Professors 19
4. A Confession by D.G. Police 21
5. The Most Potent Weapon 26
6. Shaving – A Pain that Turned into Pleasure 30
7. Better Resign from Police 33
8. Bala's Riding Blues 36
9. If You Really Love Me Darling 39
10. The Extra-Adventurous 41
11. How to Displease Your Wife? 45
12. Commit Suicide, Resign, Take Leave and Go Home 48
13. And Mr. Crawford Proceeded on Six Months' Leave to England 53
14. *Par Bhai Danda to Aap Logon ke Haath Me Hai* (But the Baton is in Your Hands) 56
15. Many a Misadventure 59
16. Tactfulness 63
17. *Sale Sahab Ki Shan Me Gustakhi Karta Hai?* 68
18. *Talwar Uthana Chahe Na Aaya Ho, Colonel To Ban Gaye* 72

19. *Yeh To Apni-Apni Intelligence Ki Baat Hai* 75
20. There is no such Officer in this Department 77
21. *Sher Ka Shikar* 81
22. *Badmuzanna Basilsile Vazarat Tark-Sakunat Kar Gaya Hai* 84
23. After All It is Democracy 86
24. *Beta! S.P. Sahab Kya Bathroom Me Hain?* 89
25. A D.I.G. with Big Mustachios 93
26. Confounded 99
27. Secret of Magisterial, Judicial and Commission of Enquiry 103
28. *Bina Padha-Likha Bhoot* (An Illiterate Ghost) 111
29. *Teen Tabarra-Madhe Sahiba, Machchar-Khatmal, Tikona-Samosa* 115
30. A Dwarf in One's Own Eyes 119
31. Dewedy! You Have Burnt Your Boat 125
32. The Rosogulla Service 129
33. The Secret of Veiled Threats 133
34. A Case for Suspension Dole to Policemen 137
35. An Alternative Way to Become Chief Secretary 141
36. The Obstacle-Creators' Club 144
37. *Manava Kahe Guman Kare?* 149
38. Application of Law – West vs. India 151
39. Transparency in Police 157
40. Politically Inappropriate Talks on Corruption 163

# Choose Your Time and Place

"I don't mean that you should become *Brahmcharis*, but choose your time and place," thus culminated the valedictory address of the Director, National Academy of Administration, Mussoorie delivered to the probationers of the Foundational Course of 1963 batch. Although this academy is a training academy for I.A.S. officers, yet it also organizes a common Foundational Course for officers of all services selected through the Civil Services Competitive Examination. As I was selected in the I.P.S. in 1963, I had also attended this course and was listening to the Director's valedictory sermon with rapt attention. The course syllabus was eminently designed to familiarize us with the Indian social, economic, administrative and political scene as well as to make us sensitive to the aspirations, needs and sufferings of the masses; but, since the academy was administered exclusively by I.A.S. officers, the ambience of the academy was *Indian Administrator Sahib-like*. Therefore, we, the probationers, had been learning more of the *Sahibi-way* of living than the problems of the masses. The Director's parting remark had tickled our young hearts in no small measure, while it had summarized the unwritten but real objective of the course in one sentence.

On 11th July, 1963, it was a cloudy evening when I had arrived at the gate of the imposing Charleville

Hotel, which housed the National Academy of Administration. As I hailed from a village, my rustic conscience was quite surprised as well as amused to see that the only shop at the gate of I.A.S. training academy was a liquor shop. Later I learnt that this 'Madhushala' had been established there to help I.A.S. probationers to learn the all-important art of drinking without the inconvenience of going to Kulri market. The administrators of the academy (all I.A.S. officers) made no bones about their love for *Bacchus* and whenever the occasion arose, they did not fail to encourage the probationers to learn this *Sahibi-habit*. One day a Bihari probationer was buying a bottle of Black Knight when a deputy director happened to enter the shop. As the Bihari probationer started concealing his bottle from the gaze of the deputy director, the deputy director reassuringly told him, "Oh! Come on. I am also going to have one."

To the credit of these trainers, I must admit that they never differed in their words and deeds and always showed large-heartedness in so far as their teaching of choosing appropriate time and place – instead of becoming Brahmcharis – was concerned. One evening four I.A.S. officers got a *bindas* lady probationer of Indian Railway Accounts Service drunk in a room of Kutesar Castle and then made her condition so pathetic that for about a month she could sit only on a pillow in the classroom. The matter had become the talk of the academy but the administrators, in their concern for the career of the young I.A.S. officers, initiated no action against those probationers, and considered it sufficient to advise them, "Choose bearable number."

One year earlier, an I.A.S. probationer had criminally assaulted a minor daughter of a poor man living on the hill-slope behind Charleville Hotel. The then Director, with stated intent of saving the girl's honor, had hushed up the matter after advising the probationer, "Choose proper age."

The academy's untiring efforts to inculcate 'right' attitude among future rulers (I.A.S. officers) towards other services are no less 'praiseworthy'. I was allotted room no. 8 in Stapleton Hotel and one Bagchi, an officer of Indian Audit and Accounts Service, was my room-mate. Since the building of Stapleton Hotel was old and its maintenance was poor, rooms of this hotel were allotted only to officers of services other than the I.A.S. After two months of our joining, Bagchi got 'elevated' to the I.A.S. because some candidate selected in I.A.S. had not joined. Bagchi was immediately allotted a room in the Happy Valley, which was the best among the various hostels. Later one day, when he had come to meet me, he confided, "Mahesh! You know what, they (the I.A.S. administrators) tell the I.A.S. probationers privately? You are there to rule while all others are to serve." This difference between the ruler and the servant became clearer to me when I joined the Central Police Training College, Mt. Abu after completing the Foundational Course. Here the body-breaking training schedule commenced at 6 A.M. and continued till 6 P.M. and even at dinner our conduct remained under watch. Moreover, not only consumption of liquor in the police mess was prohibited but also any light talk about girls was a taboo. However, full realization of the ruler-status of the I.A.S. dawned on me only during my service later. Here I found that every department and corporation of the government is under the thumb of some I.A.S. officer either directly or through secretariat, or both. The Indian Administrative Service is a permanent and all-pervasive ruler and all other services are subservient to it. Moreover, the I.A.S. officers are accountable to none excepting themselves; as they say that the king can do no wrong.

However, I do not want to miss the opportunity of expressing my gratitude towards the National Academy of Administration, Mussoorie by withholding the fact that my days in the academy were the sweetest I ever had in my life.

□

# *Aap To Na Jaane Kaise I.P.S. Me Aa Gaye!*

"Dwivedi Ji! Aap to na jaane kaise I.P.S. me aa gaye! Aap to bilkul police wale lagte hi nahi hain." (Dwivedi Ji! How could you have been selected in I.P.S.? You don't even remotely look like a policeman.")

I have heard these two sentences from the mouth of umpteen number of persons since I joined Indian Police Service in 1963; and even now after my retirement from police, some persons do not appear to have excused me for having joined police service and keep on reminding me of this 'grave misconduct'. On hearing this remark, I get confused that the person in front of me is saying so in praise of me or he is obliquely pointing out my unfitness as an I.P.S. Officer; and whether I should thank him for his kind words or ask him to shut his mouth up. Actually, on hearing the first sentence, I often feel that he is trying to convey that "I am surprised which fool selected you in the I.P.S.? You must have heavily cheated in the competitive examination, otherwise you don't appear to possess the ability of even a peanut-seller." And on hearing the second sentence, I feel that he is trying to convey that since I am neither fat and paunchy, nor have sword-cut mustaches, nor a ferocious face, I must be a not-to-be-taken-seriously type good-for-nothing police officer.

On careful consideration, I have realized that the suspicions of these persons are not totally unfounded. I have repeatedly found 'naa jaane kaise' (for inexplicable reasons) factor affecting my life and that many good things in my life including my selection in the I.P.S. had happened 'naa jaane kaise'.

In 1957, when I had taken admission in B.Sc. in Lucknow University, I had been allotted a room in Subhash Hostel. The room next to mine had been allotted to one 'Pahalwan-chhap' (wrestler-like) fresher hailing from notorious-for-murder district Hardoi. I was happy to have been allotted a single-seated room but used to tremble at the thought of ragging by seniors. The night the group of ragging-enthusiast seniors came to my room, I had fallen ill and had gone to my local guardian's place. Finding my room locked, they proceeded to the next room and no sooner than they knocked at the door, there came out Hardoi-wala fresher brandishing a hockey-stick in his hand and shouting at the top of his voice. He made ferocious movements of the stick and started chasing them. The seniors had not even dreamt of such a grand welcome and they ran for their lives; and he kept on pursuing them till they confined themselves in the safety of their rooms. Thereafter, nobody dared to think of coming to our wing for ragging and even in other wings, seniors did ragging only after being sure that no Hardoi-wala dwells there. Thus, I had a rare ragging-free first year in the university.

I had opted for Physics in M.Sc. and the toughest paper thereof was Theoretical Physics. Dr. Vachaspati, who was our teacher of Theoretical Physics, would write such obscure mathematical equations on the black-board that rarely any of us in the class would understand its head or tail, and we strongly suspected that Dr. Vachaspati himself understood neither. So, in the final examination, I also wrote such answers to the questions in Theoretical Physics that I understood neither their head or tail; and I have reason to believe that Dr. Vachaspati would also not have understood their head or tail because he gave me 96% marks in that paper which resulted in my topping in the class and becoming Gold Medalist.

After passing M.Sc., I was looking for a job when one fine morning the Head of the Department of Physics, Dr. P.N. Sharma, called me in his impressive office and told, "I have received a request from the principal of I.T. College (an exclusively girls' institution) for a teacher of B.Sc. and intermediate classes. As it is a girls' college, she has pointedly asked for a simple (meaning thereby 'harmless') person and I have given her your name. You should go and meet her tomorrow at 9 o'clock." Thus, I got the job which was a dream of every young man. Even to this day, I wonder 'naa jaane kaise' Dr. Sharma considered me to be a 'harmless' person while I used to dream of girls 25 hours in a day.

In the competitive examination of the I.P.S., I had offered Physics and Statistics as optional subjects. During examination, I had spoiled the Statistics paper and, as was my habit, after the examination, I had given 108 marks (out of a total of 200) to me in that paper. But 'na jaane kaise' the examiner gave me 151 marks in that paper with the result that despite spoiling my interview, I was not only selected but also secured ninth position which became the basis of my allotment to my home-state, i.e. U.P.

And my becoming D.G. Police, U.P. was also 'na jaane kaise'. On my part, I had left no stone unturned to ensure that I was not given the posting of D.G. Police. During training, I was taught that official and personal life of a police officer should remain separate and I had taken this lesson to my heart literally. Therefore, whenever any of my friends, relatives, or Netas talked to me for some official favour, I used to become a stiff-necked officer, which act made enemies of most of those who approached me for favour. Further, because of my outspoken nature, I did not hesitate in pointing out weak points of my seniors in the company of my friends and colleagues. Some 'more progress-oriented' colleagues among them would carry my remarks to those seniors with added salt and sour. Moreover, I was too miserly in '*butterbazi*' and 'family-service' of senior officers. So, most of my seniors were also not too enamoured of me. During my early career, one of my real well-wishers had advised me to learn to praise seniors and their wives even if they were duffers, because, in his words, "Your Annual Confidential Report is a reflection of your personal relations with your boss and has nothing to do with your official work." But stubborn as I was, I did not imbibe the useful advice. I had also acquired the reputation of sticking to honesty and rules. Although some chief ministers do tolerate and condone D.G.P.'s personal honesty, yet no chief minister, howsoever well meaning he may be, ever tolerates a D.G.P. who sticks to rules and emphasizes honesty in the matters relating to transfer-posting of police officers. Therefore, I was 'deservedly' bypassed thrice by my juniors in the posting of D.G. Police, but on the fourth occasion, when the vacancy arose, 'na jaane kaise' I was given the assignment.

All these experiences of life have reaffirmed my faith in 'na jaane kaise'.

□

# Out of Sync Professors

I underwent training during the years 1963-65 in three renowned institutions – Foundational Course in National Academy of Administration, Mussoorie, I.P.S. training in Central Police Training College, Mt. Abu and State Police Training in Police Training College, Moradabad. All of them had a mix of departmental officers and professors as trainers. The Indian Administrative Service officers posted in N.A.A., Mussoorie were, as per their training and habit, more interested in administering rather than teaching. So, they left the uninteresting and monotonous work of teaching for the professors. The professors were well paid and highly educated but had little experience of administrative realities. Our Professor of Economics, Dr. Ramaswamy had an experience of long stints of teaching in foreign universities. During nineteen-sixties, everything including food, clothes, housing and foreign exchange were so much in short supply that the governments had to perforce encourage savings and launch umpteen number of saving schemes fixing targets of savings for each district officer. Dr. Ramaswamy, who had learnt the economics of plenty in the West and had little experience of paucity, would often burst out in his lectures, "Do you think that the country is going to progress through savings? The government should encourage consumption if they really wish the country to progress." I, who had seen abject poverty and non-availability of even essentials of survival in my village, would listen to his outbursts flabbergasted. Today I can see that his theory of enhanced consumption for progress is practicable, but in sixties, it was about thirty years too soon.

Prof. Ramaswamy was thirty years ahead in his views on romance also. He had the capability of taking semi-circular or even full-circle turns during his expositions. And switching from economics to romance for him was like swimming in the water for a fish. He would bring the bored, dozing and snoring economics class to rapt attention by switching over to body-oriented romance in films from savings-oriented economic policies. He would often, while gazing with rapt attention at the youthful lady probationers, say, "Do you think that running around trees behind a hero or heroine is love?" And sometimes obliquely and sometimes explicitly profess that love comprises kissing, hugging, snuggling, smooching and further on and on.

Again his comments on Indian films were thirty years too soon because it took about three decades for the love scenes to remain no more limited to fooling around in parks and often ended in bedrooms. In the Academy also, thirty batches after my batch, one lady probationer of I.R.S. valiantly vanished for seven days with a probationer of I.A.S. while the batch was on a trek in the mountains.

□

# A Confession by D.G. Police

I was D.G. Police, U.P. in the year 2000 and had gone for the inspection of police station Mussoorie, district Dehradun (Uttarakhand was not yet created). There I went into the record room and saw an old wooden almirah (cupboard) that was full of some old registers covered with dust and mice droppings. I expressed my displeasure on the records being kept so shabbily and asked the *Deewan Jee* (head constable responsible for keeping the records) to clean the dirt immediately and then put up some of those registers before me. After quickly dusting them, *Deewan jee* put up two registers before me. I was glancing through one of them when an F.I.R. written on 19th Nov., 1963 u/s 452/427, Indian Penal Code attracted my attention. *Chowkidar* Bahadur Singh of Forest Rest House, Kandi had lodged a complaint that during the previous night when he had left the rest house for his home, some unknown persons had entered the rest house by breaking the glass pane of the shutter of a door, which was bolted from inside. They had also burnt some of the furniture of the rest house in the fire-place. I read each and every word of the F.I.R. with such pleasure which a child gets while committing a deliberate mischief thinking that he is not being observed.

The F.I.R. related to a very romantic experience of my life, which I remembered in complete detail. On

18th Nov., 1963, I was a trainee probationer in National Academy of Administration, Mussoorie. It was an off day. After taking heavy breakfast, I along with seven other probationers had started on a trek to river Yamuna that was about 18-20 k.m. away from Mussoorie. Although a road was under construction, yet it was at a primitive stage and no vehicle plied on it; and the only means to go there was by walking on foot. It was a sunny and warm morning and since none of us had any previous experience of treacherous route and tricky weather of the hills, we had not taken food items or warm clothing other than a sweater presuming that we shall be back in Mussoorie much before sunset. After we crossed Kempty Fall, whose charm had delayed us enough, we found that the route was getting tougher. At one place, a good length of the *kuchcha* road had been swept down by rain completely. Most of us thought of returning from there instead of risking our lives in crossing it, but one Indian Postal Service probationer Vishnu Saksena, who was a dare devil, encouraged and helped us cross the fissure. Most of us could cross by holding his finger only. Thus, he had to make several rounds. Resultantly, when we reached Yamuna river, sun had started going down. We had not come across any *dhaba* or tea-shop en-route and we were extremely hungry. One of us disclosed that he had brought some *namkeen* which we all shared while enjoying the beauty of the river flowing through the Himalayan foothills. The charm of the slowly flowing river was heightened here by its apparent serenity as the place was like a valley of silence, where water flowed calmly. But Vishnu cautioned us that the serenity of water was very deceptive because last year a probationer, who was good at swimming, had jumped into the inviting water and never surfaced again. Anyway, we were all getting concerned about reaching back Mussoorie in time and so the idea of jumping into the river came to nobody's mind.

We started back soon so as to be able to cross the dangerous fissure before sunset; but that was only wishful thinking because while on our onward journey it was all downhill, on the return journey it was all uphill and by now we were dog-tired. We had hardly covered a few kilometers when it started getting dark. It was also getting colder with each passing hour. Our confidence to be able to reach back Mussoorie was vanishing. So, when we saw a village on the roadside comprising 5-6 houses, we thought of asking some villager for possibility of a shelter for the night. But no man was there to talk to. We saw a woman milking a cow and one of us proceeded to approach her. But as this young man advanced towards her, she ran into her home like a girl being chased by a mad dog. Thereafter, we dared not stay there for a moment for fear of becoming a victim of male residents' ire.

When we reached the fissure, it was pitch dark and we were hungry, cold and mortally afraid for our lives. We shouted at the top of our voices for help from anybody, whosoever might hear us, but there was no response excepting the echo of our shouts reverberating between the hills. And as it subsided, we could hear only the eerie sound of the jungle, which mercilessly added to our fear of the unknown. We had Vishnu Saksena alone as our savior, but were quite skeptical that even he would be able to get all of us through without any mishap. In fact, the patch of the road which had been washed away was extremely slippery, and any slip of the foot would have made us roll down in the deep gorge like a rubber ball. We were quite confused and uncertain whether we should risk our lives in trying to cross the patch with Vishnu's support or we should take risk of dying due to hypothermia on the road. But Vishnu encouraged us and with the help of a torch and a broken branch of a tree, he made us cross the fissure one by one without a mishap. On having crossed the fissure without anybody slipping down the gorge, we shouted with such joy as if we had just escaped drowning in mid-ocean.

Then we started trudging again towards Mussoorie. After moving a few kilometers more, we saw a *chholdari* (small tent) pitched by the side of the road in which a lantern was lit. The possibility of a man being there raised our spirits substantially and we called for help. A man came out and, on our query, told us that there is a forest rest house about a kilometer away deep in the jungle. On our offer of ten rupees, he took us there. The rest house was locked and we did not find any *Chowkidar* around there. That man told us that the *Chowkidar* lives in a village about half a kilometer away, but he would not go there because he was not in good terms with the *Chowkidar*. Then he left.

We were trembling with cold; and in our desperate situation, one of us broke the glass pane of the shutter of a door which was bolted from inside. He inserted his hand in the gap so created, moved down the shutter and we entered the building. There were two *charpoys* (small cots) inside. We desperately needed rest and warmth, so all the eight of us clustered together on them. However, we soon realized that it was not possible to bear the cold without heating because in every exposed portion of the body, our blood seemed to be clotting. So, one by one, all of us got up and then went out to collect some dry leaves. We put them in the fire-place and one of us, who was a smoker and had a match-box, lighted them. And then to keep the fire burning, we started breaking the old furniture of the rest-house and putting it in the fire-place. The furniture was enough to burn till dawn. But much before dawn, we left the rest-house to avoid being detected.

Today, I confess that I did not disclose to the station officer that one of the unknown accused persons of that F.I.R. was the D.G. Police himself! After all, which D.G. Police would like to be arraigned for a mischief committed during the initial training?

□

# The Most Potent Weapon

Entry of lady officers in the Indian Administrative Service had started immediately after promulgation of our Constitution in 1950. However, their ability to control and take work from men (their subordinates and the male-dominated public) was almost invariably doubted by everybody – more so by women. This opinion was so strong that in the Indian Police Service, their entry was banned by the government on the ground that they were not suited to perform tough police duties and there was great risk involved in facing the criminals. In the same competitive examination of the year 1962, in which I was selected in the I.P.S., one Miss Gulati had a higher score than mine. She was also gifted with more athletic body than mine. Despite her ardent requests to the government for being taken into I.P.S., she was not taken and had to remain content with a central service.

After completion of Foundational Course at National Academy of Administration, Mussoorie, I had come home (in a village in the interior). Nobody of the village had ever been to Mussoorie and everybody was curiously enquiring about my life there. When I told that there were also some girls under training who were going to become Collectors, my mother was shocked beyond belief (partly because of the unbelievable thought of a lady heading a district and,

I suspect, mainly because of her apprehension of my getting entangled with one of them); and my *Bhabhi* was so amused that she had given out an uncontrolled '*phik*' from her mouth. The thought of a lady heading a district was simply hilarious among the village people. Later, I learnt that in the services also, the women officers were generally butt of a joke or of lustful insinuations among the male officers. How deep existed this bias had become clear to me during the foundational course itself.

Mr. Jha, former Director of National Academy of Administration, had come there ostensibly to deliver a lecture and enlighten us from his experiences of long and glorious career in the I.C.S. I write ostensibly because I had found that such lectures were often arranged to provide paid opportunity to the retired officers to have some nice time in the cool climes of the hills. Since Mr. Jha belonged to the U.P. cadre, some of us, who were allotted to the U.P. cadre, had been asked to meet him informally later in the evening. As I, along with others, entered his suite of the guest-house of the academy and greeted him, I noticed that he had an impressive personage with a deep voice and great command over spoken English. Moreover, like a high-bred British officer, he was taking puffs of a cigar in an aristocratic style, whose fragrance filled the room as well as my nostrils. During those good old days, smoking cigar was indicative of high breeding; cigarette smoking was more popular among the lower-rung officers. Incidentally, there were some interesting but honorable exceptions also to this rule. Sir Harcourt Butler, who became the Governor of the United Provinces, had turned to smoking Hukkah and also dressed like Nawabs because he was enamored of the Nawabi culture. He had become so Nawabized in his lifestyle that people had fondly started calling him Nawab Butler. Coming back to the main story, Mr. Jha looked like a typical British. Like the wont of any other Indian, on seeing his British manners, I presumed him to be a very broad-minded gentleman.

Mr. Jha took command of the entire conversation immediately after we took our seats. He appeared to enjoy talking – which he did dexterously and fluently with only such breaks as enhanced the effect – as much as he enjoyed smoking his cigar, which also he did with great effect. I do not remember how he brought the conversation on lady officers and narrated the following anecdote about his experience with a lady I.A.S. officer.

"One day when I was the Chief Secretary of U.P., Miss Mittal, who had been working in the Secretariat as Dy. Secretary for quite a long period, presented herself in my office with tearful eyes and started complaining that many I.A.S. officers junior to her had been posted as the District Magistrates, but she had not been given the posting even during the recent reshuffling. I looked at her face deeply and, moved as much by her complaining eyes as by her seniority, told her that soon she would get a district charge. Then I posted her as the District Magistrate, Nainital, because it was considered to be a problem-free district.

As the ill-luck would have it, an unending agitation commenced in Nainital soon after her taking the charge. When this agitation appeared to be on the brink of turning violent, I visited Nainital. Miss Mittal came to meet me at the Nainital Club, where I was staying. She appeared to be totally helpless and hopeless while narrating the stubbornness of the agitators, and became so agitated that tears started welling into her eyes. I looked at her deeply and told consolingly,

"Miss Mittal, why do you worry when you possess the most potent weapon?"

She uttered in astonishment, 'Sir?'

"Whenever a crowd starts getting violent, you should stand on some high point before it and with a sorrowful face start shedding tears. I assure you they will all melt away in no time," was my advice.

□

# Shaving – A Pain that Turned into Pleasure

On the very first morning, after reporting at the Central Police Training College, Mt. Abu, we, the trainees, were made to stand in platoon formation on the parade ground and Mr. Spadigham, the opaque-faced Madrasi Chief Drill Instructor, had commanded us to get a close (crew-cut) hair-cut every week and a close shave every morning. Thereafter, he would examine us every morning for strict observance of the two 'commandments'. The test of a close hair-cut was that no hair should be visible outside the peak-cap ring, and the test of close shave was that the palm of the Drill Instructor should move on our cheeks without even a hint of roughness. In case his palm could feel existence of an impertinent hair sticking out on the cheek, the concerned cheeky trainee would be made to run at double to the hostel and come back running after removal of the offensive hair. In the early hours of the cool mornings of Mt. Abu, such a close shave used to be a pain in the cheek.

One of us once mustered courage to tell the Chief Drill Instructor that such a neat shave was very difficult in the terribly cool mornings of Mt. Abu. During those days, modern double-triple-bladed razors were not available for an easy and smooth shave. The Chief Drill

Instructor advised us to stretch the skin of concerned part of the cheek with our fingers while shaving. While explaining it, he also gave demonstration of the same. This made his otherwise expressionless face look very funny and we were amused beyond restraint. However, his advice proved quite helpful and the torture encountered by us in trying to make our cheeks Hema Malini-like was substantially reduced. Even now I use the same trick while shaving. And then my two-year-old grandson watches contortions of my face with unmitigated pleasure and, subsequently, emulates them in the company of his playmates. One day I noticed him making funny faces at some elders and tried to persuade him against it. His interjection was prompt and unassailable, "Why Baba? Do I not make as good faces as you do?"

During training, little had I realized that the Chief Drill Instructor's insistence to shave closely will become an addiction later. It was the first day after my immobilization due to slip-disc when I felt that a close shave was one of the three greatest pleasures of life—the other two being clean bowels and soothing bath. In fact, I had got this affliction of slip-disc after enjoying the first of these two pleasures while trying to stand straight from the commode. The tail-end of my backbone had become the focus of excruciating pain and the orthopedic surgeon had commanded my total immobilization. Resultantly, my wife ensured that I did not attempt to get pleasures other than that of clean bowels. All my pleadings to my wife to allow me to shave fell on deaf ears as she had been warned by the doctor of many serious consequences arising out of the neglect of precautions. I felt miserable on that day. However, as I showed (and also feigned) signs of improvement the next day, she agreed to allow me to shave while reclining on a side on the bed. The very first splash of cool water on my face lifted my spirit beyond measure and after the shave, I felt like having tasted the elixir of life.

Although I was quite unhappy with my wife for having deprived me of this pleasure for a day, on the hindsight, I can realize why she was so unconcerned about my loss of this pleasure. Nature has reserved the enjoyment of this pleasure for men only, as it seems to have done with regard to many other pleasures too. I am surprised that there are many men who willingly deprive themselves of this pleasure by keeping flowing beards; but the tastes of *Homo Sapiens* do differ in matters of pain and pleasure.

□

# Better Resign from Police

"*Sahab Kya Gali Khana Chahta Hai?*", Ustad (a hawaldar-rank parade instructor) warned Das, a probationer belonging to my own platoon, and my blood started boiling due to anger on his offensive words.

It was a freezing evening of 12th January, 1964 in Mt. Abu (Rajasthan) when we, 57 I.P.S. probationers, had reached there to report at the Central Police Training College for one-year-long police training. Mt. Abu is situated at a height of 3,800 feet above the sea level while Mussoorie was at 6,000 feet but the ambience of Mt. Abu in the winter evening was not much different from that of Mussoorie—empty hotels and houses in the dark dewy evening gave the same haunted look, deserted streets lighted here and there by low wattage bulbs gave the same eerie feeling that some undefined entity was on a prowl behind you, and the ever-increasing cold of the foggy night would similarly make one's blood freeze in the veins. There was, however, one great difference here and that difference laid heavily in our hearts. While Mussoorie was like heaven, where leisure and pleasure were available at one's wish and entry of pain was banned, we had heard that the police training imparted at C.P.T.C., Mt. Abu was terrifyingly unpleasant and tough. And I had the taste of it in the very next morning when at 4.45 a.m. the bearer knocked at my door with a tea-tray in his hands to wake me up. After half-an-hour came the Ustad to march us to the parade ground at the double. When my batch-mate Das did not show up till 5.45 a.m., the Ustad, who had come to take our platoon to the parade ground, started threatening as above at his door. Actually, Das suffered from two personal problems – first, that it was his compelling habit to sit long at the commode, and second, that he was hot-tempered. Therefore, very soon a day came when the Ustad not only scolded Das but also made him run round the parade ground as a measure of punishment. While coming back to the mess from the parade ground, Das kept on blurting out his anger against the Ustad, and at 10 a.m., when Mr. S.C. Mishra, Commandant, C.P.T.C. came to his office, Das followed immediately behind him. Before Mr. Mishra could settle in his chair, Das started complaining against the Ustad. In a police-training college, entry of a probationer in commandant's office without prior permission was totally unexceptionable and Mr. Mishra was rightly flabbergasted. However, maintaining his cool, he curtly told Das, "Das, this is police force where you will have to learn to live with such situations. If you can't, better resign from police." And to ensure complete flattening of Das' bloated ego, he added, "Now you get out of here and remember never to enter a senior police officer's office without prior permission."

Das' unceremonious departure from the Commandant's office remained a matter of serious but hush-hush discussion among the probationers for quite some time. Some of us fumed and foamed, but nobody could overcome the fear to speak a word openly in protest. The Commandant's words had served their purpose, which was to inculcate a sense of discipline and unquestioning obedience. Since I was a youth of questioning and protesting nature, my blood boiled at that time, but, in later life, I realized that, in order to achieve a certain goal, it is necessary for any large body of men to act in unison under one man's command: questioning may be helpful in determining the right goal but is often detrimental during the process of achieving it.

□

# Bala's Riding Blues

Janak Singh, the riding instructor, shouted at the top of his voice, 'Tarrot'.

This word (as a synonym for horse's trot) was nowhere to be found in Oxford or Cambridge Dictionary or in any other lexicon of English language, yet the probationers had by now understood that through this command, the big mustached riding instructor wanted them to give a mild kick into the belly of the horse by the spurs tucked to their riding boots and to start their bottoms jump up and down on the saddle of the horse. The horses that had been broken, trained and routinely commanded by Janak Singh, understood him more unmistakably and they turned to trot mode from walking mode immediately.

I, along with other I.P.S. probationers, had reported last week at the Central Police Training College, Mt. Abu for police training. Our equitation classes had commenced from the very beginning and today we were being taught trotting on the horse. Our thighs, which had already become hairless while learning walking the horse, had now become bruised and were bleeding at certain places. However, Janak Singh would not show any sympathy to anybody, and nobody would dare to complain or even make a mention of their hurt because that would only invite the comment 'Sissy' by Janak Singh. Off the riding ground we would vociferously speak against Janak Singh and call him a *pucca* sadist but before him, we would meekly accept ourselves as the rightful objects of his sadism. But since exceptions prove the rule, there was one probationer by the name Bala (Bala Subramanyam), who had his own plans to outwit not only Janak Singh but also the Commandant.

It was a strange combination—Bala and police. Bala loved his beer and enjoyed to while away his time in its uninterrupted '*khumar*' while police training demanded alertness even while dying of fatigue. Horse-riding was certainly an unacceptable interruption in Bala's pass-time. Therefore, the very first day Bala was to ride the horse, he came with a knee-band complaining that he had severe pain in the right knee and could not mount the horse. Janak Singh was neither impressed nor mellowed and got Bala lifted by the syces on the horse. Bala was not the one to be subdued by any shouting of Janak Singh or forced lifting of himself. So, he soon started throwing up (vomiting) on the back of the horse. Janak Singh was left with no choice but to ask Bala to dismount and stand outside the riding ground till the riding period was over. Bala's confidence grew by leaps and bounds and on subsequent occasions, he came so drunk that managing a 'throw-up' proved to be a left hand's job. Janak Singh got so frustrated that he no more shouted at Bala or even asked him to ride the horse. Having gained that much ground, Bala discovered that standing by the side of the riding ground for full 60 minutes was too much of an interruption in his '*khumar*' and he totally stopped coming to the riding ground. Janak Singh reported the matter to the Commandant, who directed the Asstt. Commandant Mr. G.A. Burge to ensure Bala's presence during riding classes. Burge sent repeated notices to Bala, which were put to good use by him by throwing in the fire-place to keep the room warm. Then, one day, Burge came to the riding ground and finding Bala nowhere there, he ordered four hefty probationers and a syce to lift and bring Bala from his room. The troupe went and on Bala's refusal to come to the riding ground, they lifted him from the bed forcibly. Bala immediately conjured the old trick and started throwing up on all of them. Disgusted, they put him back on the bed and took hasty retreat. On hearing their report, Burge, despite his anger on Bala's defiance, could hardly suppress his smile. Thereafter, everybody gave up and Bala was no more asked to come to learn riding. Of course, he was given a big 'Zero' in the equitation examination.

After the completion of the training period at C.P.T.C., Mt. Abu, Bala joined the State of Orissa, to which he had been allotted. According to the service rules, failure in any subject meant repetition of examination each year at the time of the examination of new batch of probationers. Rules also provided for withholding any increment and promotion till the clearing of examination in that subject. The Orissa Government sent him thrice to Mt. Abu to clear the riding examination and Bala came back undaunted with a big 'Zero' scored each year. Ultimately, the poor Gvernment of Orissa wisely thought it better to not waste money on Bala's horse-riding and exempted him from further riding tests. Bala became the first S.P. in the history of Indian Police, who never passed a riding examination.

□

# If You Really Love Me Darling

During training, visit of guest lecturers was always a welcome change in our otherwise tough and exacting routine. This was particularly so because we had come to know that the guest lecturers, who generally used to be retired or serving senior officers, often spoke on subjects which would rarely be asked in the examination – so we needed not tear our brains on what they spoke. Secondly, if the guest stayed for the night, then his visit meant enjoyment of a guest night in the mess in which lady wives of the staff members also participated in an otherwise male-alone police mess. This was also an occasion for listening to personal experiences narrated by the guest lecturer and some impromptu cultural program. Some of those occasions became so interesting or funny that I still remember them well.

One day one Major General Singh of the army had come as a guest lecturer. During his lecture, he spoke and spoke but I could not know what he spoke excepting the fact that before each noun, he used the four-letter word as an adjective after adding 'ing' to it. This was a blasphemy in our atmosphere and since it was being committed in the presence of the Commandant, it made his lecture hilarious for us. In the evening, during guest night, he wisely kept his mouth shut because his language would have offended the ladies beyond measure as he was incapable of uttering a full sentence without inserting that word before every noun.

Therefore, the trainee officers were asked to fill in the gap by singing some song or narrate some joke. One Verghese of the Kerala cadre sang the following song which soon turned into a chorus because other trainees could not stop singing along with him.

"If you really love me darling, don't come at one,
Papa would be waiting darling with a double barrel gun,
With a double barrel gun.

If you really love me darling, don't come at two,
Mummy would be waiting darling, with a wet leather shoe,
With a wet leather shoe.

If you really love me darling, don't come at three,
Uncle would be waiting darling, with a three-not-three,
With a three-not-three.

If you really love me darling, don't come at four,
Aunty would be shouting darling, chor, chor, chor,
Chor, chor, chor.

..........................................................................................
..........................................................................................
..................................

..................................................don't come at ten,
..........................................................................................
.................................."

It amused us so much that it became a sort of anthem for us and whenever an occasion arose, we would egg-on Verghese to sing it and everybody would clap and sing along with him.

□

# The Extra-Adventurous

It was a hot afternoon in Gujarat at Palampur when we were stranded in a chartered train at the railway station. All the probationers were being taken on an 'euphemistically called' educational trip from Mt. Abu to Goa. The truth was that everybody including the officers of the Central Police Training College, who had arranged the trip, knew without an iota of doubt that the trip was primarily a pleasure trip with education, if any, being a by-product. Today, such a trip may seem a small affair, but in those days when half the Indians could hardly afford both meals a day, it appeared to me to be a great luxury—although very dear one because I was one of the enjoyers of that luxury. Though we were entitled to travel first class, yet we were travelling sleeper class because of non-availability of first-class coaches for our chartered train. Since this train was out of the routine schedule, it was allowed to proceed further from a station only when normal traffic had passed. The train had halted at almost every station falling on its route and at the Palampur station for such a long duration as if it was the culmination of its journey.

Soon we started losing our cool and the initial euphoria of the journey to Goa started fading. After waiting for about half-an-hour, some of us started hurling the choicest of abuses at the non-present railway administration. We derived some vicarious pleasure in those abuses and our nerves got somewhat soothed. So, some of us made ourselves long on their berths and started dozing and others indulged in small talk. None of us had any inkling that there was an extra-adventurous probationer among us who had started getting restless no sooner than the train started showing signs of a long sojourn. He was a tall, sturdy, and macho-looking fellow. Suddenly, he got down and went to the enquiry-counter where he was told that the train will halt for four hours more there. He came back and smilingly updated us about the train's late schedule. Then he left immediately telling us that he was going to the town and would be back before the departure of the train. And he did come back huffing and puffing just when the train's engine had started huffing and puffing and its wheels had started creaking. After the signal had turned green, some of us had started worrying about him and seeing him come back at the nick of the hour, we were greatly relieved; but looking at his appearance, we were highly astonished. His hair were standing on his head, his shirt was torn and face was red. We were naturally curious and as the train gained its speed and the probationer settled himself, we started questioning him about where he had gone and what had happened. As he tried to avoid giving straight and believable answers, we started smelling rat and, therefore, pestering him more and more. Having been cornered from all sides, he came out with the truth. His story was the juiciest one that any of us could have dreamt of. He told that after getting out of the railway station, he had hired a rickshaw and had directed the rickshaw-puller to take him to the red-light area at double speed. Poor rickshaw-puller was no connoisseur of 'available' beauties and had little knowledge of any popular red-light area. However, he knew one 'available' woman living in a *jhuggi*. He took him to the *jhuggi* and introduced him to the woman who was also tall, sturdy and of macho-looks. The probationer neither had a choice nor was very fastidious in his tastes. Further, the price was very reasonable and affordable. So, he happily agreed and eagerly started the proceedings. However, the poor woman's rickety cot could not bear the delightful thrusts of two heavy-weights and broke down during the process. On conclusion of the encounter, the woman vehemently demanded rupees twenty extra as the cost of the cot. The probationer had not catered for that. So, a brawl ensued and when the probationer attempted to leave the *jhuggi* without paying the full amount, the woman caught hold of his hair in her right hand and his shirt in her left hand. The probationer called the rickshaw-puller, who was waiting outside, for help. But he was in for a surprise because, instead of helping the probationer, the rickshaw-puller became an accomplice with the woman. They emptied his pocket, tore his shirt and also some of his hairs before he could extricate himself and run at double towards the railway station.

In our young and fertile imagination, the whole incident was so hilarious that none of us complained thereafter when the train stopped for long hours at scheduled or non-scheduled stops. Instead we would start egging on the probationer to go to the town and repeat the performance.

This probationer was allotted to the Odisha cadre and I was allotted to the U.P. cadre. I was least surprised when, two years after we had parted, I heard that this A.S.P. had been suspended for having made physical overtures to a lady passenger sitting in a bus by his side. But as is the norm in government services, the suspension was soon revoked and the officer continued to indulge in his amorous adventures and climbing promotional ladder undaunted.

□

# How to Displease Your Wife?

Mr. B.R. Gupta was one among my batch of seven I.P.S. officers allotted to U.P., who had come to Police Training College, Moradabad for State-Police Training. Having availed age-exemption for appearing in the selection test because of his emergency services in the Air Force, he was 7-8 years older in age than most of us. He had been married before entering into the I.P.S., but had been living alone during one year's training at Central Police Training College, Mt. Abu. It was compulsory for the probationers to live in the mess and entry of any woman in the probationer's mess was totally prohibited excepting on guest nights which were held once in a blue moon. The women had not yet been permitted to join the I.P.S.

On 13th Jan., 1965, when we reached P.T.C., Moradabad, its officer's mess was already full as two batches of Dy. Ss.P. were already undergoing training there. Therefore, all of us were accommodated in one wooden-floor hall which used to be a ball-room dance hall during the British period. I was elated on learning that this mess has had the privilege of being a training institution for I.P. officers also during the British Raj. Each of the probationers was provided with a paid bearer, whose duty was to bring tea in the early morning, wake us up in time for the morning parade, and help us in our routine chores. However, one duty secretly given to the bearers by the authorities was in the knowledge of none of us – and that was to keep unobtrusive watch on our activities and report them quietly. After a few days of our stay, one night, when I woke up, I found that Mr. B.R. Gupta was not in his bed. I thought that he must have slipped away for some uncontrollable nightly performance. In the morning, Mr. Gupta had entered his bed before the arrival of the bearer. The next night again he vanished from his bed but had not returned when the bearer brought the tea. None of us could answer the bearer's query about Mr. Gupta's bed being empty. Mr. Gupta came a little later and was courteously offered tea by the bearer. He was also on time for the parade. This emboldened Mr. B.R. Gupta and he started returning after the bearer's arrival almost daily in the morning. Soon he was summoned by the adjutant in his office to explain his absence from the bed in the mornings. Initially, he kept mum, but soon found that his silence was being interpreted as a nocturnal visit to not-so-well reputed places. Having found himself cornered between the devil and the deep sea, he – with tears welled up in his eyes – confessed that he had invited his wife from his hometown in Punjab and was keeping her in a rented room in the city. The adjutant was not too pleased to learn about this 'serious' infringement of rule and retorted,

> "Proceed to that room immediately, put your wife on the first available train to Punjab and report compliance by this evening."

Mrs. Gupta was furious on her husband for having called her first and then putting her in an unreserved coach to travel back to Jallandhar. She stopped replying to his letters also which was the only solace available to the lovelorn heart of Mr. Gupta and we found him in a fairly depressed state during our next two months' stay at Moradabad.

Now whenever we meet, we jokingly ask Mrs. Gupta to narrate the incident in detail. And from the expression that comes on her face, I guess that the scar is not completely wiped out even today.

□

# Commit Suicide, Resign, Take Leave and Go Home

"Do you know why I am here?" Then without waiting for or even expecting a reply, "Because the Principal is out on tour. But that does not mean that things are not well under control. When the Principal is out on tour, I hold the fort and when I am on tour, the Principal looks after my work," was the introductory statement of the 'venerable' Vice Principal of Police Training College, Moradabad to our class. I harbour a gut feeling that anybody with rotund body and a rounded, hairless, shiny top has got to be 'venerable'. The Vice Principal, whose flesh was filling every cubic centimeter of the office chair and leaving much to spare, had started the class by thus imposing his authority, which, as was apparent on his face, seemed to add an aura of venerability around him. Despite the awe, some of us could hardly suppress our smile – which was fairly broad despite our efforts to the contrary – on hearing the last sentence of his authoritative statement.

On having completed the training at Mt. Abu, the eight I.P.S. officers allotted to the U.P. cadre had come here only the day before for training in state laws and state practices. And this was our first class in the P.T.C. After his introduction, the Vice Principal came out with another weighty statement,

"The first lesson that I wish to teach you is that you should forget all that you have learnt at Mt. Abu and remember only that which you will be taught here."

Now this was too much for us to digest without a hearty laugh because our main training centre was C.P.T.C., Mt. Abu, where we had undergone a tough and thorough police training for one full year and here we had come for only 10 weeks for familiarization with U.P. State's special laws and practices. Thereafter, the Vice-Principal told us many things about the futility and impossibility of doing the police work successfully while adhering to the laws and rules. Later, in our career, all of us were to realize the truth inherent in the teachings of the Vice Principal. Everybody concerned with the criminal justice system – complainant, policeman, advocate, judge and the accused – know it that, in most of the cases, neither the F.I.R. lodged by the complainant, nor its investigation by police, nor evidence produced by defense counsel, and not even the judgement is based on the whole truth. In fact, the bias of the laws and rules in favor of the accused and standards of our adherence to the truth and morality are such that any investigation and trial of a case based solely on laws and rules is –saving rare exceptions – bound to result in letting the criminal go scot-free.

Unfortunately, the persons administering such a criminal justice system hesitate to speak openly about the weaknesses of the system – more so, in a police training college. Instead, conscientious police officers, prosecuting officers and judges try to overcome these weaknesses and get results by not always adhering to the impracticable laws and rules. The fact that the venerable Vice Principal was only speaking the truth dawned on me soon when I was posted as circle officer, Phulpur in district Allahabad. The S.S.P. had received information that during the previous night, a person had entered a house to commit theft in a village in police circle Sarai Mumrez, but the villagers woke up and he was done to death while fleeing. The S.S.P. asked me to proceed to the village, conduct enquiry and take necessary action. During enquiry, the innocent villagers stated with a sense of pride that they had killed the thief while he was fleeing. I had been taught at C.P.T.C., Mt. Abu that if a thief enters somebody's house during night, then it is no crime if the thief has to be killed to prevent crime within the confines of the house. But if the thief comes out of the house with intent to flee, then killing him will amount to an offence of 'culpable homicide not amounting to murder'. So, armed with the knowledge of Indian Penal Code thoroughly imbibed at C.P.T.C., Mt. Abu, I felt a sense of achievement while getting a case of 'culpable homicide not amounting to murder' registered against the villagers on the basis of their own statements.

In the evening when I returned to Allahabad and was proudly reporting the facts to the S.S.P., he interjected,

"What? You got a case registered against the villagers?"

Without reading anything in between the lines of his interjection, I replied, "Yes sir. They had killed the thief while fleeing."

Although otherwise a suave officer and a gentleman, the S.S.P. could not control his outburst,

"*Maine apni zindagi me itna ch**** police officer nahi dekha hai.* (During my whole life, I have never seen such a silly police officer.)

I was at my wit's end.

Having uttered that the S.S.P. terminated the meeting abruptly. Then the next day he called me and told calmly,

"I am sorry for my words, but you have to realize that if the villagers will be prosecuted for facing the criminals, who will come out to save the victims of dacoities and burglaries in the villages."

I did realize that I deserved the rebuke for failing to imbibe the first lesson of the venerable Vice Principal that adherence to laws does not necessarily result in good policing.

During his remaining lecture, the Vice Principal maintained such a poker face that I am yet to discover how much serious or humoristic he was when he concluded his lecture by the following sermon,

"Soon you will be posted as a Superintendent of Police of a district. Remember that control of dacoity (armed robbery by five or more persons) is very important for a Superintendent of Police; and, if a Superintendent of Police cannot control dacoity, he should commit suicide, resign, take leave and go home and do it strictly in that order."

A year later, as circle officer, Phulpur, district Allahabad, I discovered that the knowledgeable Vice Principal might have been hinting at learning some novel ways of controlling dacoities. In a circle neighbouring mine, dacoities had become very frequent. The S.S.P. expressed his displeasure to the concerned circle officer. The circle officer ran around day and night but dacoits ran faster than him and the number of Special Reports of dacoities kept on increasing. So, the clueless circle officer proceeded on two months' leave. The S.S.P. ordered that the charge of this circle be taken over by a veteran circle officer Mathura Singh. And lo and behold, from the day Mathura Singh took over charge of this circle, the number of reports of dacoities came down to almost zero. The S.S.P. apparently felt relieved, but I was beyond my wits to understand the magic wand applied by Mathura Singh which appeared to have turned all dacoits into *sadhus*. One day during a gossip session of circle officers, I lauded the achievement of Mathura Singh and asked him about the extremely effective steps taken by him. He seemed to have smiled at my childish query, and told patronizingly,

"Give me any circle, and I guarantee control of dacoities within two days." Having said that he excused himself and after his departure I repeated my query to another veteran circle officer. This circle officer's disclosure was revealing,

"Mathura Singh is known far and wide among police officers for immediate control of dacoities. No sooner is he given charge of a circle, he calls all the Station Officers (S.O.s) and tells them in no uncertain terms that he hates seeing a special report of dacoity; when he sees the first, he will recommend award of adverse entry to the S.O. and on second report, he will get the S.O. reverted. Thereafter, no F.I.R. of a dacoity is written at the police station. Even in a dacoity accompanied with murder, the report is written u/s 460 I.P.C., which is a crime defined as committing murder while having entered a house at night with intent to commit theft."

This revelation made me understand why no Superintendent of Police commits suicide, resigns, takes leave and goes home even when the dacoits make hay in the sunshine of police laxity.

□

# And Mr. Crawford Proceeded on Six Months' Leave to England

Mr. B.N. Lahiri, I.P. (Retd.) had come to deliver a lecture when I was under training at Police Training College, Moradabad. He had served under British Raj for almost the entire duration of his career and, after independence, had become the first Indian I.G. of U.P. He had a razor-sharp memory and outstanding gift of gab. He was also a compulsive narrator of anecdotes of his police career, which he was deservedly proud of. He had delivered an enlightening talk to our class during the day time. So, we were keen to hear him again during the guest night, which was held in his honour. And he did narrate an anecdote, which tickled our hearts for long.

British were very particular about selection of I.C.S. (Indian Civil Service) Officers and usually brilliant graduates of the reputed universities only could pass the tough competitive examination. But since they wanted a repressive police force in India, they nominated (later selected) as I.P. officers such spoiled brats of powerful British families, who would not study beyond Senior Cambridge (11th class). Mr. Crawford, I.P., was a shining example of this British policy. He was S.P., Allahabad in the year 1924. He was a chronic bachelor, but was a keen connoisseur of the pleasures of life. His standing instruction to his orderly was to put one bottle of whisky with soda on each corner of his sprawling bungalow's huge drawing room before the clock struck 7 in the evening. Then he used to walk like a caged tiger in his drawing room and whenever he reached any of the four corners, he would take a gulp of the whisky to warm up his body as well as soul. He was fond of holding gala parties at his residence in which he would invite all Englishmen of the town – more emphatically if one had a pretty wife.

One night when such a party was in full swing and Mr. Crawford as well as the guests had gulped enough whisky from the bottles placed at all corners of the drawing room, Mr. Crawford extended his hand to request the lovely wife of an Executive Engineer to dance with him. She promptly accepted the invitation. The candle light dance provided an ideal opportunity to Mr. Crawford to transfer the heat of his pounding heart to that of the lady. And his gaze kept on penetrating her heart so deeply that it started yearning for physical union. Then how could Good Samaritan like Mr. Crawford wait to apply soothing balm to such a heart!

Mr. Crawford had always considered it 'infra-dig' (below his dignity) to go to his office for any official work and used to spend office hours at his bungalow itself. In fact, he also considered it 'infra-dig' to do any official work except signing such papers which could not be disposed of without his signature. But now he so altered his routine that as soon as the clock struck 10 a.m. and the Executive Engineer would leave his residence for office or for site, Mr. Crawford's jeep would enter his bungalow to stay there till just before the lunch-time when the Executive Engineer returned.

Thus, Mr. Crawford was having whale of a time in the company of the Executive Engineer's wife. But as they say, *'ishq aur mushq kabhi chhipte nahin hain'*, the Executive Engineer got scent of the liaison soon. So, the next day while leaving for office, he locked his bungalow from outside. That day Mr. Crawford met with an unbearable disappointment when he had to return without meeting his sweetheart. In that state of frustration, he sent a telegram to the I.G. Police (at Lucknow),

"The P.W.D. Executive Engineer has wrongfully confined his wife in his bungalow. Request permission to register a criminal case against him and break open the lock to free his wife."

The I.G. knew Mr. Crawford too well to have acceded to his request. Instead he found out about the scandalous overtures of Mr. Crawford from the Executive Engineer and sent back a telegram,

"Mr. Crawford! You proceed on six months' leave to England immediately, failing which you will be transferred to district Ghazipur."

Since every Englishman used to tremble in his shoes on hearing the name of the malaria-infested district Ghazipur, so without giving a second thought, Mr. Crawford applied for six months' leave. And he proceeded to England – but, of course, with the wife of the Executive Engineer.

□

# *Par Bhai Danda to Aap Logon ke Haath Me Hai* (But the Baton is in Your Hands)

At the time of my selection in the I.P.S., I had told my elder brother, who was an accounts officer, that I must have missed I.A.S. only by a few marks. Upon this he had smilingly replied that he was happier for that and had narrated a very interesting incident. An insincere but talkative sweeper woman used to come to his house for cleaning the bathroom. One day on noticing that the bathroom was not properly cleaned, my brother rebuked her for her carelessness. She promptly retorted,

*"Hame na gussa dikhaio. Hum tum se nahi darti hain. Tum ka koi sipahi ho jo danda jadak diyo?* (Don't show me your temper. I am not afraid of you. Are you a constable that you would hit me with your *danda* (baton)?"

I had had a hearty laugh on hearing this, but during my police career later, I found that ordinarily people care for the words of those only who wield a *danda* (baton) in their hand. They also serve them with devotion. Mr. Sumitra Nandan Shrivastava, an advocate friend of Basti district, had once very succinctly put this point in the following words: "Although Police gets people punished and we advocates save them from punishment, yet public regards police much more because in this country, Shankar Ji is the most worshipped *Devta*."

So all departments of the government remain in constant competition to keep their *danda* fatter than that of any other department and this competition is at its zenith in revenue, police and judicial departments.

This *danda-sanskriti* prevails in the minds of officers as much as it does in the mind of the sweeper woman. Some officers even remain on a lookout for an opportunity to belittle other departments and, frankly speaking, I was no exception to that due to some adverse initial experiences in police service. In the month of March 1965, after completing training at P.T.C., Moradabad, I was posted at Jhansi for field training. Here I used to play badminton in the Jhansi club with a trainee P.C.S. officer and a young Munsif Magistrate. One day I heard the P.C.S. officer and the Munsif speaking in my presence.

"What does the S.P. think of himself? He got a circular issued by the district magistrate that the D.I.G., Kanpur range (then Jhansi was part of Kanpur range) is coming to Jhansi and he will stay in the inspection house for three days. Officers who wish to meet the D.I.G. may call on him at the inspection house. *Arey, hum to jab chahen D.I.G. ko court me summon kar sakte hain* (Hunh! We can always summon the D.I.G. in our court)."

I felt greatly hurt on these exclamations of such junior officers against an I.P.S. officer of 22 years' seniority. Gradually, I learnt that even senior officers of a department get vicarious pleasure in belittling other departments and exaggerating their own authority. Although the truth is that no officer's authority is any authority against others unless it is misused; if used according to rules, every authority is merely a duty. The authority to issue summons by a court is similar to authority of a traffic constable to stop any vehicle for checking or authority of a station officer to arrest anybody including a magistrate reasonably suspected of having committed a crime.

Another incident which deeply affected my mind is of the year 1977. An I.A.S. Officer of the rank of Divisional Commissioner was enquiring into the tragic incident of collapse of the bridge on Saryu river in Ayodhya during a fair in which many persons were drowned. I happened to reach the P.W.D. inspection house to meet this Commissioner when he was unburdening his heart before the district magistrate like this:

"*Jab se engineers ka character roll likhne ka adhikar D.M. se le liya gaya hai, tab se in salon ke dimag bahut kharab ho gaye the. Ab dekho sale kaise pichhe pichhe nach rahe hain* (since the authority to write Annual Confidential Report of the engineers had been taken away from the D.Ms., these engineers had become totally unbridled. Now, watch how they are dancing around me."

Display of such meanness even by a senior officer made me extra-sensitive about the comparative thickness of my department's *danda*.

During my training, I was told that after my posting in a district as A.S.P., I should call on the S.P., D.M., Judge and Civil Surgeon. So, in Jhansi, I had gone to call on the District Judge, who was a very frank and friendly person. Our conversation had somehow turned towards the prestige and protocol among district officers. And in the end, the District Judge had blurted out with an involuntary sigh, "*Par bhai danda to aap logon ke hi hath me hai.*"

□

# Many a Misadventure

Adventurism is a compulsive lure of the youth, but adventures of the youth are quite often a consequence of ignorance than of bravery. Police career provides innumerable opportunities for adventure and I also indulged in quite a few in my youth – particularly during field training of police.

In the year 1965, I was posted at Lalitpur, which was a Tahsil of district Jhansi, for field training. It had hilly terrain, but was a dry region with little rain. It abounded in natural beauty because of hillocks and bushy forests, in poverty because of scarcity of water for crops, and in brigands because of inaccessible rocky terrain. There in the jungles of Lalitpur lived Kabutari Nuts, who had been branded a 'criminal tribe' during the British period. Most of them still continued their age-old tradition of training their male children in thefts and female children in bootlegging. There also roamed gangs of dacoits (brigands), who consisted mostly of such villagers who had fled into the jungle as outlaws after committing murder(s) to take revenge of some real or imaginary injustice done to them or to some of their family members. After killing the so-called persecutor(s) and running away from law, they thought that they had become *Baghis* (rebels). In the jungle initially, they joined some established gang of *Baghis*, and later, some of them rose to become gang leaders themselves. I, being totally ignorant about their methods, habits and habitat, had indulged in quiet a few misadventures during training.

One fine morning I was told by some villagers that the Kabutari Nuts residing in a certain forest were regularly indulging in bootlegging and committing burglaries with impunity because the police station staff was mixed up with them. I was also told that I can find illegal liquor and wherewithal for making it any time in their houses. I decided to raid their houses without informing the police station. So, I proceeded to the village along with two constables in my jeep. I had hoped to catch some of them red-handed while distilling liquor and also to recover some stolen property from their houses. However, what actually happened I had not bargained for. On seeing the police jeep, all the men of the village ran away to take cover in the thick of the forest and the women and children numbering in scores came out of their huts and collectively started shouting and abusing us. Some of them started dancing obscenely and others were prepared to confront us with sticks and bricks. We were not only outnumbered but were also totally unprepared against such an organized feminine resistance. Moreover, there was possibility of the menfolk returning after coming to know our lack of strength. Use of lethal force against such a congregation of women and children was out of question. The driver of my jeep quietly advised me to retreat at the moment and come later with more force. I saw wisdom in his words and went back empty-handed and white-faced. So, the first raid of my career had ended in our hasty retreat. On having come to know of my misadventure, the experienced circle officer advised me to never confront Kabutri Nuts' families without due preparation, because their womenfolk were well trained in not only confronting the policemen but also in making false allegations of violating their modesty after tearing their clothes or of arson after burning any of their abandoned thatched-roof huts.

Another incident of my 'fearlessness' turned out to be of no less unwise dare-devilry. I was attached to a rural police station in circle Lalitpur for a week. As there was no other place to stay in that police circle, I had to stay in a forest rest-house located at a lonely place by the side of a hillock. I had been married only the previous month and I could not suppress the temptation of taking my wife Neerja with me there. Since Lalitpur circle was infested with *Baghis* (brigands) and its jungles were their haven due to terrain-provided security, the circle officer had detailed a section of P.A.C. (nine jawans) for our protection. We had reached there in the scorching summer afternoon, but it had started cooling down fast at sundown. On our arrival, we had seen a small temple under a huge banyan tree at the top of the hillock. The evening breeze enlivened our spirits and we decided to visit the temple. I asked my orderly to accompany us and we proceeded bare-handed. By the time we reached the temple, it had started getting dark. We got lost in the romance of the night at the hilltop and returned only after the orderly advised us to return soon because brigands often visited this temple in the evenings. And lo and behold! We had not descended the hillock even halfway, when torches started switching on and off around the temple. Later, I was told that the brigands were only waiting for us to leave. We had escaped capture because unlike today, during those days, the criminals – weak or strong – invariably avoided confrontation with the police.

During this attachment to the rural police station, I was also expected to do night patrolling. One night I took the station officer and half section P.A.C.

(four jawans) from my camp-guard in my jeep and started for the patrolling duty. My wife refused to stay alone at night and accompanied me on the same jeep. She has a hawk-eye for spotting wild animals in the jungle and was as much absorbed in looking for them as we were looking for dacoits. After about two hours of patrolling, we reached Dudhai forest rest house where I asked the driver to stop the jeep so that we could use its toilet. We found no Chowkidar there, but to our utter surprise, we found the door of the rest-house open and a fire burning in the hearth. The S.O. told us that almost certainly there was some gang in the rest-house which had melted away on seeing the lights of the police jeep. So, to our chagrin, I and my wife discovered that those rest-houses provided shelter and comfort not only to the government officers but also to the *Baghis* after their tortuous and torturous journeys in the forest.

□

# Tactfulness

In common parlance, tact means wisdom that enables one solve an intricate problem with least adverse effects. But the administrative vocabulary has its own meaning of tactfulness. Here it means solving a problem without any regard for truth, laws, rules and self-respect in such a way that the powerful gets satisfied and the powerless keeps his mouth shut. In the Indian conditions, this is the *Moolmantra* of success for police and administrative officers. Tactfulness has been a potent tool of administration since medieval period in the Indian history. During the Moghul and British period, this was called 'Hikmatamli'. Rulers and ruled both like tactful officers, who may or may not do their duty, but must put so much sweet in their tongue that the ego of the listener gets inflated like a balloon. Due to a long history of subjugation, our capacity to digest glaring untruths and hypocrisies is almost unlimited, while our digestion for any bitter truth is very weak.

By temperament and upbringing, I am an animal of tactless kind. This 'suicidal for success' trait of mine had become clear to me during my first job as a lecturer in I.T. College, Lucknow. My father's ex-classmate Mr. Tripathi had written a letter to me recommending the name of a student for awarding high marks in the examination. Instead of succumbing to the illegitimate demand which Mr. Tripathi had made considering it as a matter of right or declining it with a reply laced with sweetness of *chashni,* I had tersely written back that this was against my principles. And I was 'deservedly' reprimanded for the same by my father as Mr. Tripathi had complained to him for having offended him. In the end, my father had advised me "even if I did not want to award undue marks, I should not have written back that it was against my principles". Out of respect for him, I had kept quiet but, living in that romantic idealism of the youth, I had not inwardly agreed to what my father had advised. Today I realize that had I accepted my father's advice unreservedly, I would not have earned the displeasure of so many friends and relatives of mine during my career and would not have made enemies of a horde of politicians, bureaucrats and others.

I had the taste of consequences of failing to listen to my father's advice during my first posting as S.P., i.e., of district Pilibhit. The students of the Ayurvedic College, Pilibhit were on strike demanding equal status to their degrees with that of M.B.B.S. The Health Minister had planned a visit to Pilibhit. Some *Netas* belonging to S.V.D., the minister's party, came to meet me and asked for foolproof security arrangements for the minister as there was apprehension from the Ayurvedic College students of creating trouble. I told them that necessary measures would be taken, but some of them were not satisfied and kept on insisting that great caution is needed to ensure that the minister's public meeting passes off without any kind of interruption and no black flag is shown to him. Their hankering on the same point got me lose my cool and I retorted,

"How can police prevent if some students bring small flags in their pockets and start waving them during the minister's address?" Then I added,

"After all it is democracy."

The *Netas* did not take kindly to my straightly stated truth and later complained against me to the minister, alleging that I were a *Congressi*. The minister was only too willing to believe his party-men's words and had a very weak digestion for any bitter truth – particularly spoken by a suspected *Congressi*. I was soon shunted out of the district.

Riotous situations demand quick, firm and tactful handling because any delay in controlling them may lead to loss of life and property as well as serious consequences to the career of the concerned police officers. Unfortunately, here too tactful does not necessarily mean straight, truthful and impartial. The flame of riots is often fanned by spreading rumors which may or may not have any factual basis. During the assembly election of 1974, I was S.P., Saharanpur, where the most contested election was between the Congress candidate Mr. Kultar Singh (younger brother of Shahid Bhagat Singh) and a Muslim League candidate. Muslim League was desperate to create a foothold in U.P. and had enough support – particularly among substantial Muslim population of the city – to give a tough fight to the Congress candidate. For the Congress candidate, the money and liquor were being spent like water by a Sikh who controlled the liquor trade of the district. Although it will be difficult to say which party was violating the rules more blatantly, yet one thing was clear that Muslim League was out to create a communal situation so that the Congress supporters among Muslims fall for it. A Hindu lad indulging in Holi festivities provided them the desired opportunity when he threw color on a bearded Miyan Ji and on his abusive reaction, roughed him up with the help of his co-revellers. The Muslim League people jumped to take advantage of this minor incident and spread a rumor that a Maulvi had been done to death by Holi revellers. The Maulvi was persuaded to lie on a cot which was taken out in an ever-lengthening procession to the police station. The tempers were running high among the crowd which demanded immediate arrest of the 'murderers'. When I came to know of this, I reached the office room of the police station. The inspector, who had become aware of the true facts, apprised me of the situation and told that the only way to calm down the largely ignorant but fuming crowd was to show arrest of some persons. He further added that he had already sent some constables to catch hold of some poor persons to show to the crowd that the 'murderers' had been arrested. When these 'arrested' persons arrived, I stood on a stool and delivered a speech on historical tradition of Hindu-Muslim unity in Saharanpur and declared that the culprits were already in police custody and could be seen by any two-three persons from the crowd. This pacified the crowd, which started melting. The ring leaders among the crowd were left with little option but to become quiet, and soon they lifted the cot on which 'dead' Miyan ji was lying and moved out of the police station. Later, the sentry told us that no sooner the retreating procession reached about hundred yards from the police station, the 'dead' Miyan ji had come down on his feet and started walking with the crowd. Later, we offered tea and biscuits to the 'arrested murderers' and explained the necessity of their being brought to the police station. They were only too pleased for not having been actually booked for murder and were astonishingly grateful for having been offered tea at the police station. Everybody was pleased for our tactful handling of the grave situation and thumped our back, and nobody admonished us for having violated the law of the land by unlawfully detaining those persons.

In a situation where widespread riot has broken out, the most desirable thing to do is to control it quickly by hook or by crook and it has been observed that riots are not controlled by being too judicious and too impartial but by suppressing one of the two warring parties and, unfortunately, the weaker one is always easier to suppress. So, the police often applies this tact for bringing back peace and saving loss of life and property.

Tact is the most useful tool in making a criminal confess his crime. The less a police officer has to resort to third-degree methods in exposing the riddles of a crime, the more tactful he is. The 'tact' may include long and sustained interrogation, keeping the suspect awake for long hours, making him sentimental by fake show of sympathy, or offering pouches of *Desi* to make him float in seventh heaven. Physical torture may be a necessary tool in breaking criminals in cases like kidnapping, terrorism, etc. where time is of essence in saving lives, yet a tactful officer should avoid its use as far as possible.

Since tact is of tremendous importance in police work, there is no use saying that it is an equally rare trait. It is to some extent inborn, but mainly an acquired trait. Therefore, it should be included in the training syllabus of all police and administrative officers. Although the dividing line between tactfulness and dishonesty often gets blurred, in today's conditions, tactfulness is the most desirable trait for success in a policeman's career.

□

# Sale Sahab Ki Shan Me Gustakhi Karta Hai?

To uphold the *Shan* (bloated prestige) of one's *sahab* is considered a religious duty among the government servants – particularly in administrative and police services. This devotional feeling among the subordinates emanates with a design to keep their bosses pleased and indulgent so as to allow them to indulge in open loot of the exchequer as well as the public. If someone has had the privilege of staying or visiting the camps set up for D.M., S.P., and judges in all too frequent *Melas* and exhibitions, one could not have missed the ferocity of the competition in lavishness and wasteful expenditure in setting those camps—particularly revenue officials think that their job is at stake if the D.M.'s camp is found to look less magnificent than that of any other camp. Since the introduction of Air Conditioners in the senior officers' posh bungalows, no district officer likes to stay in those camps, yet there has been no let down in the competition on the expenses in establishing them. They are often not visited by the bosses even for as many minutes as the number of thousands are spent in establishing them.

In the very beginning of the career of senior officers, their subordinates—particularly in police, administration, and judiciary – effectively cultivate their minds so that they start believing that the prestige of the *Sahab* is upheld by keeping *Sahabi-Rutba* rather than by public service. I can never forget the way one station officer had upheld my *Rutba* and took advantage of the same in the beginning of my career.

During the year 1966, I was posted as A.S.P. i/c circle Phulpur in Allahabad district. The S.S.P., Allahabad received a complaint of non-registration of a case of theft by the S.O. of Police Station, Phulpur. The enquiry into the complaint was entrusted to me and one morning I proceeded straight to the place of enquiry, which was in the *kasba* Phulpur itself. On learning of my arrival in the *kasba,* the S.O. 'dutifully' came to meet me at the place of alleged theft. Since the complainant was a poor man, his house had no prohibitive shutters in the doors and many days had passed since occurrence of theft, I did not find any clue to conclude either way about the reality or otherwise of the incident. At the time of my enquiry, there was only a boy of about 17-18 years age present in the house who, on my asking, confirmed the occurrence of the theft while the S.O. alleged that it was a trap to implicate his enemies. As the boy spoke too fast, I could not follow him fully and started cross-questioning him on some points. And that gave an opportunity to the S.O. which he was eagerly waiting for. Due to his immaturity, the boy, instead of giving straight answer to my questions, got emotional and blurted out,

"You, such a senior officer, cannot understand even this much..." and before he could proceed further, the cunning S.O. slapped him saying, "*Sale Sahab ki shan me gustakhi karta hai*!"

Instead of intervening, I watched this *karastani* of the S.O. as a bystander for two reasons – one, that I was equally immature as a police officer and had myself felt insulted on the wordings of the boy and second, that I had been taught not to rebuke a station officer in public lest he lose his control in his area. Thereafter, it had no meaning to ask anything from the boy because he had got terrorized and was sobbing uncontrollably. Finding it to be an opportune time, the cunning S.O. suggested that I should proceed to the police station where he would call all the witnesses and since I had to complete the enquiry soon, I agreed.

At the police station, there were umpteen number of witnesses – some of them considered respectable in the society – who stated that no incident of theft had taken place and this complaint was only a ploy of the complainant to implicate his enemies. Till today, I firmly believe that these witnesses were tutored ones, but I had to send a report to the S.S.P. that no evidence of the occurrence of the theft could be found.

The S.S.P., who was not only an honest officer but also had a reputation for his brilliance as a police officer, made a 'Seen File' noting on my report, which in administrative jargon means that no further action is called for. One evening during light conversation, he started telling me,

"Dewedy, you know that despite our serious efforts to the contrary, almost all the station officers indulge in non-registration and at least 30% crime is not being registered in the district. The theft had actually taken place in the case in which you had given a report that no evidence could be found about the occurrence of the theft. But what can be done? If true reports are submitted in all complaints, then all the station officers would be under suspension and nobody will be left to do police work."

Even today after my retirement, I feel guilty for having kept my mouth shut while the S.O. slapped the boy apparently to maintain my *Shan*.

□

# *Talwar Uthana Chahe Na Aaya Ho, Colonel To Ban Gaye*

"*Talwar uthana chahe na aaya ho, colonel to ban gaye*"—my father-in-law, who was S.S.P., Agra, had aptly remarked when I got promoted as Commandant 23rd battalion, P.A.C., Moradabad within one year of my posting as circle officer. By that time I had completed only three years and three months in the I.P.S., out of which two years and three months had been spent in training. Although my father-in-law had said it humorously, the truth of his observation dawned on me soon after joining the new assignment. I was only 25 years old then and younger in age and experience to most of the officers and men I was expected to command. In military-like regime, being the senior-most officer, it was not expected of me to take guidance from subordinates in routine matters. So, I started learning from hearsays and clichés—and the first lessons that I learnt were these:

1. *Commandant ko apni battalion me seenk khadi karke rakhni chahiye* – which meant that a commandant should keep an atmosphere of his terror in his battalion.
2. Commandant should maintain tight discipline in the battalion – which, in my understanding, meant that I should generally support all actions of the senior officers against their subordinates.

At that time, both 23rd and 24th Battalions situated near village Harthala in Moradabad were newly created battalions and most of the constabulary of those battalions was temporary. As the luck would have it, soon after my posting in 23rd Battalion, a new commandant was posted in 24th Battalion. He had a tendency for such compulsive adherence to '*seenk khari karke rakhna*' that he would discharge every constable reported against for even very minor misdemeanors. Within a few months of his arrival, he scored half a century in discharge orders. As these hapless men were temporary, according to the then existing rules, no departmental proceedings were necessary before issuing the discharge order. When I saw that his *seenk* was standing too erect, in order to keep semblance of equality, I also discharged five constables.

On retrospection, I realize that I had got all the wrong notions about keeping the *seenk* straight and maintenance of discipline in the battalion. I had awarded *dalel* (extra fatigue) to an outshining constable on receipt of a minor complaint against him. Probably, he had not committed any act of misdemeanor because he did not comply with the order of doing extra fatigue and appeared before me with an application that he had not committed any mistake and, therefore, was not willing to do the *dalel*. I was not willing to revisit my order of minor punishment. Upon this, he put an application that he may be discharged from the service as he was not willing to comply with the Commandant's order. I thought that revising my order then would encourage indiscipline in the battalion, and without speaking a word with him, I ordered his discharge. In another case, I dismissed a Head Constable from the service on the complaint of an Asstt. Commandant that the Head Constable who was working as Mess Havildar had misappropriated some wheat flour. After dismissing him from the service, I learnt that the Asstt. Commandant concerned was no doyen of virtues and could have faked the complaint against the Mess Havildar. And on witnessing the fact today that the officers misappropriating crores of rupees become 'apple of an eye' of the ministers and, instead of being dismissed, are given most lucrative assignments, I think my act of dismissing the Head Constable was an epitome of immaturity and heartlessness.

I am of the opinion that the posts of Commandant, S.P., D.M. which are loaded with authority should be given to officers only after they have learnt properly to hold the *talwar* (sword) and use it appropriately.

□

# *Yeh To Apni-Apni Intelligence Ki Baat Hai*

Shri Babu Ram Sharma was the adjutant of 23rd P.A.C. Battalion when, in 1966, I was promoted and posted as Commandant of this Battalion. He had attained the rank of Dy. S.P. from that of Sub-Inspector and was nearing retirement. Occasionally, he used to become too outspoken before me for three reasons – one that he hailed from Meerut region where people are not particularly famous for mincing words, two that he was about to retire and three that he presumed that he had a right to take some liberty with me because he belonged to my caste, i.e. Brahmin. One day he entered my office, saluted and told,

"Sir, I want to go to Garh for inspection of our Battalion's contingent deployed there. My village is a few kilometers away from there. If you permit me, I shall make night halt in my village instead of Garh."

I had reservations in permitting him to take official vehicle to his home village and so told him,

"How can I permit you to take official vehicle to your village and make a night halt there while on official duty?"

The adjutant unhesitatingly replied,

"Sir! I have to stay overnight somewhere. If I stay at my village, I shall be able to look after my home problems too."

I was mulling over the matter when Sharma added a bit impatiently, "Sir, *Isme harz hi kya hai? Yeh to apni apni intelligence ki baat hai.*"

I permitted him without delay because denial of permission would have put a question mark on my intelligence. Later, I discovered that such intelligent use of official opportunities for doing private work simultaneously was a norm in government service, and I also started using my intelligence 'intelligently'.

As I rose in rank and gathered more experience of the working of our administration, I discovered that top officers and ministers rarely made any distinction between an official tour and a private tour. Senior officers often visit capital towns like Lucknow or Delhi 'officially' for getting a desired posting or for cancellation of transfer order. When I was I.G. Gorakhpur, the then P.M. used to fly frequently to his hometown Ballia from Delhi to attend private social functions like *mundan* or marriage ceremonies.

□

# There is No Such Officer in this Department

On Oct. 3, 1966, I had been promoted to the rank of S.P. and was posted as Commandant 23rd. Battalion P.A.C., Moradabad. My ego had got bloated beyond measure due to the fanfare with which I was received by the ever-disciplined and ever-ready-to-please men of the P.A.C., the sprawling bungalow that was Commandant's residence, and a suddenly dawned knowledge that inside the campus of the battalion 'I was the monarch of all I surveyed'.

There was another great relief in posting at Moradabad that my immediate boss Mr. R.C. Gopal, D.I.G.-P.A.C. had his office 340 k.m. away in Lucknow. He was reputed to be fond of speaking in contrived British accent and I was hardly able to express two straight sentences even in Indian accent. However, as I could easily pose to be an ideal dumb listener, I felt rather relieved when I was told that he felt exhilarated while narrating to Commandants (the captive audience) about his ex-army career during the Second World War, in which he was captured by the Germans. I met him next month in the Annual Commandants' Conference at Sitapur. Here I learnt from fellow Commandants that he was very keen on smart looks of Commandants. During sixties, parallel trousers of fifties had become outdated and quite tight-fitting trousers had become fashionable. It was a common belief among the Commandants (although nobody claimed to have had personal experience) that during inspection of the parade, Mr. Gopal's measure of Commandant's smartness depended upon the refusal of the trouser to allow a soda-bottle to enter it when inserted from the bottom. On my first interview with him, Mr. Gopal asked me a baffling question,

"Dewedy! You know why you have been posted under me?"

I had not had the faintest idea and looked at him askance. Then having enjoyed my ignorance-born discomfiture for quite a while, he disclosed,

"So that you become smart."

I did not consider anything amiss in it because I really was rather rustic in my dress, demeanor, as well as in thoughts. Some of my batch-mates who had exhibited more smartness during their tenure as circle officer were posted directly as S.P. i/c of the district, instead of being given such a side posting like P.A.C., intelligence, etc.

I remained posted in P.A.C. for two-and-a-half years: and in retrospect I guess that I had belied the hopes of Mr. Gopal and had not become smart yet, because thereafter I was posted as S.P., Intelligence Department in Lucknow instead of S.P. i/c of a district. I had come to Lucknow in the sweltering heat of June 1969. There was no house (only temporary accommodation in M.L.A.'s flat courtesy my uncle-in-law who was M.L.A.), no cooler (A.C. was an unseen commodity), no vehicle (not even a jeep), no orderlies and no guards. And at the top of this, the boss D.I.G.-Intelligence was ever present in the office to call, advise or scold me at any time he so pleased. When I reported my joining to him the next day, I was half-expecting that his first question will be,

"Dewedy! You know why you have been posted under me?"

And after enjoying my discomfiture leisurely, he would answer the question by declaring,

"So that you become intelligent."

However, Mr. H.K. Kerr, D.I.G. – a man of few words – did not ask this question. And its reason was disclosed to me during lunch hour by another S.P., Mr. M.D. Dikshit, who had been there for many years. There were three S.P.s at Intelligence Headquarter and all of us took lunch in his room, because he was seniormost and had a beautiful terrace attached to his room on the first floor. With a mischievous smile in his eyes, he asked me about my first interview with the D.I.G. I was feeling miserable right from the time I had arrived in Lucknow and was bursting to unload myself. So I told him not only about my interview with D.I.G. but also about the question that I was half-expecting and my surprise that it did not materialize. Mr. Dikshit appeared to be thoroughly amused on my expectation as he told,

"There is a serious reason why this question was not put to you. When Intelligence Department was newly created, an urgent secret letter was to be dispatched to its head by a *Babu* (clerk) of the U.P. Government Secretariat. But this *Babu* had no idea of the designations of the officers of this newly created department. In good faith and with malice towards none, he addressed the envelope to,

'The Intelligent Officer,
Intelligence Department
1, Gokhle Marg,
Lucknow'

The *Babu* of the Intelligence Department, who received this envelope, was totally foxed to see the address. As the envelope was marked 'SECRET', he dared not open it and returned the envelope to the secretariat with the following note on it,

"R.I.O. (returned in original) with the remark that there is no such officer in this department."

□

# *Sher Ka Shikar*

In the government service – and particularly in the administrative services – officers are very conscious of their postings. On each new posting, they compare it with the posting of other officers of their seniority and feel elated or let down accordingly. However, there are two types of officers – one who measures the category of posting of a particular district by its size, budget and administrative problems and the others who measure it by the size of their bungalows, number of available cars for personal use, lack of administrative problems in the district, and availability of *shikar* in the jungle. The former considerations are for better opportunities for career enhancement and may also be for one's enrichment while the latter are for peace, creature comfort and romance of the jungle. During British Raj, Windham, District Magistrate of Mirzapur, had earned so much popularity through his indulgence with the wild and its inhabitants that no Collector seems to have ever surpassed. He continued to hold charge of Mirzapur district for thirteen long years. I also had a preference for the latter between the two and, as the luck would have it, got first district charge of Pilibhit where forest was only eight kilometers away from S.P.'s bungalow.

*Shikar* was not yet prohibited by law. On the contrary, the government itself used to allot blocks of forests to rich people for *shikar* at a price. *Shikar* of a tiger was considered to be an act of bravery and a desirable quality in a D.M., S.P. and D.F.O. The then District Magistrate Chandra was a friendly I.A.S. officer two years senior to me in service. He had already earned the reputation of having shot a tiger while combing the forest on a tractor. Although some persons had their misgivings about this claim and some of his batch-mates on hearing this news had commented that 'Having seen Chandra, the tiger must have died laughing', Chandra enjoyed that reputation. He became my friend, philosopher and guide in *shikar* and on most of the weekends, our families used to spend nights at *machans* arranged with the help of a famous *shikari* named Bharat Singh. They used to be great outings. We would leave the jeep on the road and ride on elephants to reach the *machan* stealthily as well as to climb on the *machans* straight from the back of the elephant without having to climb the tree. A buffalo calf was tied near the tree to allure the tiger in the silence of the night, which used to be eerie, hair-raising and romantic. Bharat Singh had taught us to keep completely silent while waiting for the tiger. He was also a great story-teller and before the commencement of *shikar* would narrate his adventures of *sher ka shikar* in finest details. He proudly claimed to have killed 65 tigers in his life. On hearing some rustling sound or a cry of a barking deer, he would enhance the nightly romance by telling us in hush-hush tone to remain alert for the kill. Along with our hair, our ears would also stand erect and eyes would pop out to see the tiger. When the rustling sound would die out, Bharat Singh would wait for a while and come out with the oft-repeated explanation that the elusive tiger was too smart and had left the place having smelt our presence. Then he would call the *mahouts* to bring the elephants and we would come back home in the early hours of morning.

For our nightly labors, Bharat Singh would praise us for having spent the night on *gasht* in the dacoit-infested forest. Besides Bharat Singh, there were many others too, who would buttress our ego on our night-outs by speaking highly of our efforts to control dacoities. However, the general public was not too impressed by our labors. Some youngsters got particularly annoyed with the D.M. and spread unflattering rumors against him and also pasted posters branding the D.M. as *shikari*. Soon he was transferred, but, being son-in-law of a senior I.C.S. officer, was given charge of district Kheri, which had more *shikar* in it than Pilibhit.

I could not earn the epithet of '*Sher ka Shikari*' (tiger-shooter) not because of any lack of desire on my part but because of my wife Neerja's abhorrence in killing any living being. She is a strict vegetarian but an unstoppable lover of the wild. She possesses astoundingly keen sense for spotting wild animals in the bushes, but is absolutely no-no on allowing me to raise the gun towards any of them.

□

# Badmuzanna Basilsile Vazarat Tark-Sakunat Kar Gaya Hai

Urdu was the *lingua franca* of the lower hierarchy of the police department in northern India during British period. After independence, it was replaced by Hindi but for many decades Urdu terminology continued to be used at police stations – although, in Hindi script, Urdu, having been the court language for centuries, is extremely sophisticated and is capable of expressing a lot in a few words and with great punch.

And so it expressed in the Village Note-Book of a certain village in district Deoria. For each village falling in the jurisdiction of a police station, a village Note-Book is maintained at the police station in which among other things a year-wise history of history-sheeter criminals is maintained. For each hardened criminal, who is declared history-sheeter by the S.P., a separate page is allotted on which the Station Officer makes annual entry regarding his criminal activities during the year. In Deoria district, there was a habitual cattle thief whose history-sheet had been opened. As the 'democracy' would have it, he contested M.L.A.'s election and won. Pulling his caste strings, he also became a minister and, in order to perform his ministerial duties, started living in Lucknow.

It was no joke for the Station Officer to award an entry in the history-sheet of a criminal, who had become a minister. However, the Station Officer exhibited exemplary courage as well as great literary genius in writing the following annual remark in this minister's history-sheet:

"*Badmuzanna basilsile vazarat Lucknow ko tarksakunat kar gaya hai. Philahal khamosh hai, par uske mazi ka khayal karte hue sakht nigarani rakhne ki zaroorat hai.* (The bad character has migrated to Lucknow in connection with ministerial duties. Presently, he is quiet, but keeping his past in view, close watch is needed on his activities.)"

Of course, the Station Officer did not last long in the district.

□

# After All It is Democracy

Pilibhit was my first charge as S.P. It was also first occasion for any political party other than Congress to rule the state of U.P. I was posted there in Jan. 1970 when a coalition government formed by Sanyukta Vidhayak Dal was in power. I and the *Netas* of Sanyukta Vidhayak Dal were equally new and inexperienced in the art of administration. Rough edges of neither of the two had been smoothened. Moreover, each constituent political party of this conglomeration of parties thought that the government officers continued to remain pro-Congress and anti-Sanyukta Vidhayak Dal. Being a Brahmin, I was a natural suspect because Brahmins, Muslims and Dalits had been ardent supporters of Congress throughout.

In my boyhood, I had naively cultivated a false notion that goodness means frankness and tactfulness essentially means pleasing by deception. I did not realize that in India the quickest way to lose friends and make enemies is indulging in the luxury of tactlessness of telling the unpleasant truth on somebody's face. So, I had become a compulsive tactless person. As I could rarely withhold the truth whatever its nature, my interaction with *Netas* often led to unpleasant consequences.

The students of Ayurvedic College of Pilibhit had been on strike for quite a long time demanding parity of their degree with that of M.B.B.S. One fine morning when I was working in my residential office, some persons belonging to Bhartiya Kranti Dal came to see me. They told that the Health Minister was visiting Pilibhit, next week and there is likelihood of the students of Ayurvedic College trying to disturb his programs. Therefore, detailed police arrangements should be made during his stay here. I said O.K. Due to my brief reply, those ruling party leaders thought that I were shortchanging them and one of them started rather haughtily,

"*Kaptan Sahib, dekhiyega ki koi ladka jeb me kala jhanda laakar meeting me naa dikhane lage.* (S.P. Sahib, do ensure that no student brings black flag in his pocket and starts waving in the meeting)."

The tone and words both were too much for me to swallow and I retorted,

"This type of protest cannot be prevented – practically as well as legally. After all, it is democracy."

Those *Netas* belonging to the main ruling party had never dreamt of such a forthright reply and left in a huff. So, on the minister's arrival, they made a mission of their lives to make him convinced that I was a '*pucca Congressi*'. The minister's meeting passed off peacefully but, as ill-luck would have it, the minister made an unscheduled visit to one of his friends' house in the evening. Some Ayurvedic College students were keeping track of his movements and soon others gathered there and started demanding a meeting with him. On refusal by the minister, they started shouting slogans and dancing around his car which was parked outside. Policemen accompanying the minister were insufficient to handle the swelling crowd. At about 8 p.m., the minister phoned me at my residence that the students were not allowing him to come out of the house and were breaking his car. During those days, the police in Pilibhit was limited and so was its mobility.

Therefore, instead of ordering reinforcement from police lines, I readily took three constables of my house-guard in my jeep and proceeded to that house. When I was about 50-60 yards away from the house, I saw that the policemen outside that house were few and I also had only three policemen with me. Luckily, a plan flashed into my mind. I asked my driver to stop the jeep there itself but keep its head-lights on and focussed straight on the students. Then I told that everybody in the jeep would get down together and run towards the students shouting at full throat, *"Pakro-Maro, Pakro-Maro......"* This *"Pakro, Maro, Pakro-Maro..."* tactics worked because in the darkness, the students could not see us or guess our real number. They thought that a big force had arrived and was charging upon them. They ran helter-skelter in panic for their safety. Thus, we got opportunity to deploy the available policemen properly to prevent their regrouping in the street and the minister could get away safely.

However, the minister, whose ears had already been poisoned against me, on his return to Lucknow, took no time in complaining to the Chief Minister about my being a 'staunch *Congressi*', and I was promptly ordered to proceed to Central Police Training College, Mt. Abu for a six months' refresher course of training. Thus, I learnt that 'the democracy's rules were not for a ruling party'.

□

# *Beta! S.P. Sahab Kya Bathroom Me Hain?*

"*Kutta malik ke liye bada wafadar hota hai, par dusron par gurrata hai.*" A *Miyan Ji*, who was sitting on the berth just opposite mine along with his large family, blurted out these words unexpectedly without looking at any person, as if he was addressing the air. On this sudden outburst, I started looking at him, and felt that perhaps I was the target of his remark. Although I felt a bit uneasy, yet kept quiet because I had no idea of the context. Then *Miyan Ji* started pouring out his *bharas* (frustration) about constables' behavior with his family members. And gradually the reference and context of his *bharas* dawned on me.

During 1965, I was posted at Allahabad and within a few months of my posting, I had an appendicitis attack. My father-in-law, who was S.S.P., Agra, asked me to come to Agra for operation. During those days, there used to be 1st, 2nd and 3rd classes in railway coaches. I was not in a condition to travel in 3rd class and first-class travel would have upset my budget. As there used to be no reservations in the 2nd class, the practice was that whoever earlier occupied a seat or a berth by spreading his hold-all became the owner of that space for the entire journey. Of course, passengers arriving later would often cajole, plead, threaten and quarrel with him to share the space occupied by him. '*Yeh bhi koi sharafat ki baat hai*?' used to be the common refrain before commencement of full-throated quarrel and those who could speak in English would soon turn to it in order to make the opponent speechless as well as to subdue him by invoking his inferiority complex. Depending on one's sensitiveness, physical weakness and degree of inferiority complex, one would make space for the other or continue to occupy his space boldly. In order to get a berth reserved for me (by way of occupying first), I had sent two constables in advance to spread my hold-all on some vacant berth. When I reached the station, they had fully spread my hold-all and were conventionally occupying the entire berth for me. I took off my shoes and made myself comfortable on the berth. Soon the train whistled and the two constables saluted me and alighted from the train. Although everybody was watching the proceedings, yet nobody uttered a word until the constables left the coach. Then the *Miyan Ji* started blurting out his anger, although in the air and indirectly. Soon some other passengers also joined him in enhancing my knowledge of the publics' opinion of the police behavior. Then I realized that I was the target of their diatribe. Being a very thin-skinned person, I started feeling ashamed of myself and as I was mulling on the idea of rolling back my hold-all to make way for some members of the *Miyan Ji's* rather large family, the T.T.E. entered the coach. After checking my ticket, he demanded tickets from the *Miyan Ji* and it turned out that for his six passengers, he had only three tickets. He had presumed his two children apparently aged 6-8 years to be below 5 years entitled for free rail travel and had not bought any tickets for them; and he had bought only half tickets for the other two of 15-16 years' age presuming them to be considered below 12 years by the rail authorities. The customary argument and counter-argument between the T.T.E. and *Miyan Ji* commenced. The *Miyan Ji* pleaded, cajoled and invoked the *Sharafat* and *Insaniyat* of the T.T.E. with intent to save the charges but the T.T.E. stood to his ground threatening to take penal action. The entire coach got so engrossed in this new drama that my constables' misdemeanor was completely forgotten. I took out the *chadar* from my hold-all, covered myself head to feet and slept unabashedly till morning when the train steamed into the Agra station.

The elephantine hold-alls which almost every traveller worth taking notice of used to carry in the trains had its victims from all strata of society – the old and infirm coolies, the unwary bystanders, the carefree children and the late coming passengers who panic and run without any controls. Sometimes the heavy hold-alls of the heavy-weights did not spare even the police officers. One night a Superintendent of Police posted in P.T.C., Moradabad travelling in a first-class coach from Moradabad to Lucknow was suddenly awakened as a heavy hold-all had been thrown on his feet. As his senses became aware of the circumstances, he found that the train was at the Bareilly Station and there was a commotion created by fleeing and shouting policemen. When he tried to express his displeasure, a fat and strong policeman growled,

"Yes! we shall soon shift the hold-all." And then either to impress the passenger or in his self-defense added, "It is C.O. Line's hold-all."

The suave S.P. thought it wise to meekly fold his feet and quietly watch the proceedings. He discovered that a passenger who was to alight at the Bareilly Station and whose berth was to be occupied by the 'venerable' C.O. Line was still asleep and the confused constables had thrown his hold-all on the S.P.'s feet.

During his subsequent police career also, this C.O. Line turned out to be an officer of great '*Phun-Phan*' which was then regarded to be the most desirable quality in an effective policeman.

No police officer would have ever become such a miserable victim of the hold-all as a young I.P.S. Officer who had come to join as S.P. Rampur on his first promotion. The C.O. city and Inspector Kotwali had come to receive the new S.P. at the Railway Station after donning their well-starched uniforms and well polished medals. No sooner the train halted, they entered the first-class coach in a huff pushing aside a teenager-looking young man standing at the door of the coach. They found only one hold-all lying on a berth which was vacant. Finding that there was no other person in the coach, they asked the teenager-looking person,

"*Beta! S.P. Sahiab kya bathroom me hain*?"

'Beta', who was S.P. himself, had no words to answer.

□

# A D.I.G. with Big Mustachios

I had not taken her seriously when my one week old wife Neerja had, during a serious conversation, casually remarked,

"People flaunting big mustachios cannot be very brainy persons because their intellect comes out of their head and rests in their mustachios."

I had not only disbelieved her but had also felt offended because in my younger days, I also used to keep mustachios (medium-sized) which I used to straighten off and on, and then twist them at the ends to make them look like those of Dev Anand in '*Hum Dono*'. When she realized that I was taking her remark to be a caution against my sword-like mustachios getting bigger and thicker, she clarified soothingly,

"This observation is not my own but that of my Papa (who was also an I.P.S. Officer), who had a sixth sense of assessing people's personality correctly. He had come to this conclusion after observing the behavior of quite a few of his relatives and colleagues, who sported big mustachios."

Although I have never admitted it to my wife, her remark was one of the reasons among others of my saying good-bye to my well-nourished and well-flourished mustachios later in life. However, the strongest reason for this painful parting with my mustachios was not her remark but my posting as S.P. Basti under Mr. Ram Singh, D.I.G., Gorakhpur range. Mr. Ram Singh was a British-timer policeman; and he was also a match in *gora* color and handsome looks to many British officers.

I had received the D.I.G.'s program for annual inspection of my district; and he arrived in the evening dot at the given time. He was scheduled to stay at Basti for two days. During those good old days, annual inspection of district used to be of great importance for S.P.s; and preparations regarding office records, crime reports, investigation results, prosecution of cases, etc. were given as much importance as those of white-washing of office and residential buildings, of piloting, escorting, receiving, feeding and keeping in good humor the D.I.G.

I am not revealing any secret of the administration by confessing that no district officer likes a very hard-task master type of inspecting officer and I was no exception. I had received the D.I.G. at the P.W.D. inspection house with as smart a salute and as loud clicking of my heals as I could manage. I was quite impressed to note that the response of the D.I.G. was no less smart. Actually, he appeared to overshadow even the guards in smartness when he was presented with a guard of honor. I was getting overwhelmed and overconscious in dealing with such a smart D.I.G. His mustachios, which were double the size of mine and more straight than mine, were poor consolation. In fact, they were only further unnerving me. However, one trait of the D.I.G. gave me an inner hint of his not being such a hard-task-master; and this was his unstoppable habit of enjoying every free moment of his life in twisting his mustachios.

After the D.I.G. had visited the lavatory, settled down in the massive sofa and the initial formalities sugarcoated in flattery like 'I hope the journey was not too tiring Sir', 'Thankfully the weather is quite pleasant Sir', etc. were over, the orderly dressed in a freshly washed shining white dress brought tea in a freshly washed shining white tray. The properly trained orderly served the tea first to the D.I.G., and then to myself in accordance with the protocol of our ranks. The Dy. S.Ps., R.I., Inspr/Kotwali, and a dozen other police officers were waiting outside for any of them could be called for any question relating to work or, more likely, for any arrangement of personal comfort to the D.I.G. Their ears were standing erect like that of a rabbit lest any of them miss to hear the call at the first stance. Although the older and experienced among them were comparatively relaxed, the younger ones were on the verge of wetting their pants [frankly speaking, I did not check anybody's but I strongly suspect that the fidgety young Dy. S.P. (under training) would have found it hard to keep his trousers dry].

Unlike his external demeanor, I found the D.I.G. to be rather chatty, because once the tea slipped into his throat—dexterously bypassing his thick mustachios—he started talking about *shikar* (big game like tiger, leopard, etc.) and enquired about its availability in the district. I would have loved to say 'yes'; and I hated it the most to tell him that although Basti was full of forest during British days, now there does not exist any forest big enough to support *shikar*. I had expected some disappointment on the face of the D.I.G., but I could not see even a trace of it when he spoke,

"Oh, it's immaterial. I have had enough of *shikar* during my police service. In fact, when I was S.P., Etawah, I had even kept a tiger as a pet."

I was more amused than impressed to hear that, because that seemed to me to be the most effective way of keeping scores of '*Fariyadis*', who swarm the S.P.'s residence right from early morning, at bay.

However, apparently I said (as if surprised and overwhelmed),

"Really Sir. That is fantastic."

My expression must have created an impression of extremely keen interest in listening to the story of Tiger-Pet, because thereafter the D.I.G. kept on narrating every detail of it so incessantly that it was only after about an hour that I could manage to interrupt him to extend invitation of dinner at my residence at 8 p.m. The D.I.G. thankfully accepted and as only about an hour was left before dinner time, I took my leave hurriedly before he could resume his narrative of the ferocious pet.

For dinner also the D.I.G. was punctual to the dot. This punctuality again unnerved me a bit because he had arrived at my residence before any other guests – D.M., Judge, C.M.O., etc. – had come, and I thought that he might not feel particularly pleased about this. I received him and requested to sit on the main sofa where an *'Angithi'* was kept in front to keep him warm. I sat by his side on another sofa. The D.I.G. soon made himself comfortable and restarted the story of the pet tiger from the point it was left untold at the P.W.D. inspection house. However, before he could make much headway, the D.M. arrived. The two of them greeted each other, and soon after the D.M. had made himself comfortable, the D.I.G. told that he was narrating the story of a tiger whom he had kept as a pet during his posting as S.P., Etawah. Then in order to keep the D.M. abreast, he restarted the story from the very beginning. And then as other guests kept on coming, he restarted it quite a few times for the 'benefit' of each of them. The constipation caused by over-consumption was getting writ large on some faces, when my wife tactfully intervened and announced the dinner. We moved to the dining room and the dinner was eaten in comparative peace.

However, after the main course was over and we had moved back to the drawing room, the D.I.G. picked up the lost thread without waiting for the coffee. After the coffee was over, other guests started excusing themselves because it was getting late in the wintry night. The D.I.G. stopped in between only to say good night to them. After the last guest had left, the host (myself) remained the only audience, who was as much captive as submissive. So the pet tiger's story continued until late night and ended only after the tiger died of constipation despite vet's untiring efforts to loosen its bowels.

I was totally exhausted by the time the D.I.G. left for the inspection house and was mortally afraid that during the long-drawn inspection next day I might fall asleep. Next morning I was woken up early by my wife because the D.I.G. was scheduled to inspect the parade in police lines. He came as punctually as ever, inspected the parade and appeared quite pleased. Then I went home and glanced through the pile of files on my residential office's table before proceeding to office for inspection. The D.I.G. came, went to each and every room of the office, spoke pleasantly to the staff and then took the inspecting officer's seat. I put files of police buildings, crime, prosecution, etc. before him for his perusal. He opened one of them. I was looking at him with trepidation because he had picked up the dacoity file whose number was fairly large in my district. Then to my surprise he asked,

"Dwivedy, have you not prepared an inspection note for me?"

I had not expected this because I knew that inspection note is dictated by the D.I.G. to his C.A. The D.I.G. noticed my consternation and added,

"Don't worry. You write it at your leisure and send a copy for my signature."

And then the inspection was over. Subsequently, I sent a draft inspection note to the D.I.G., which he signed and issued. Only alterations that he made were for adding a few clauses in my praise.

One day when we were exchanging pleasantries, the veteran D.M. asked me,

"How did your inspection go?"

On hearing the details from me, he had a hearty laugh and told,

"You really earned those praises by hearing him so patiently. However, this is nothing as compared to the story of a British-timer I.C.S. officer who was Commissioner of Varanasi division. He had inspected Gorakhpur district (during British period, Gorakhpur was within the jurisdiction of Varanasi division) for seven days. He remained busy in *shikar* for all the seven days and never went to D.M.'s office for inspection. After his return to Varanasi, he sent an inspection note, which read as follows,

"I went for inspection of Gorakhpur district and stayed there for seven days. I had inspected this district last year also, and written an inspection note. I have nothing to add. The D.M. is very familiar with each block of the forest area of the district and (therefore) he is doing extremely well."

I asked the D.M., "Did the Commissioner sport big mustachios?"

"Oh! He did and loved to twist them," the D.M. replied smiling heartily.

□

# Confounded

A completely drenched poor young woman in tattered clothes was standing before me and I was feeling dumbstruck. I was S.P. of district Basti. The bungalow of S.P., Basti is situated at the bank of river Kuano, a fairly big seasonal river. I was disposing of files in my residential office when this woman was brought by Inspector Kotwali in that cloudy morning. She wore such an opaque 'mask' on her face and looked so blankly in the vacuum that nothing could be read either from her face or from her eyes.

With intent to make her conscious of her present situation, I looked straight at her eyes and asked, "What is your name?", but could not notice any movement in her stony eyes. Then I looked at Inspector Tripathi and asked,

"Was either of the children found?"

Tripathi replied, "Sir, despite our best efforts, none of the two has been found."

On hearing this her body moved slightly and then she slumped at the place where she was standing. Slowly, tears welled up in her eyes and, after a while, she started wailing,

"*Haay! Hamar bachawa, hamar lal! Tu hamka akel chhod ke kahan chale gaiyu* (Oh, my son...my darling...where have you gone leaving me alone?)...*ham aapan bachawan ki hatyarin han. Hamka mar jai deo* (I am a murderer of my sons. Let me die...)."

Her wail was so pathetic that it was making tears brim in my eyes too. When she had wept enough, I again asked her,

"What is your name?"

She looked at my sympathetic face and muttered, "Bhagwanti."

I asked, "Where do you live?" and she replied, "Mahripur."

Then I put the real question, "Why did you do it?"

Having heard my question, she seemed to have been lost in her past for some time; and then, sobbing in between, narrated her story as follows:

She belongs to Balmiki caste. She was married in village Mahripur eight years back and two sons were born to her within five years of marriage. Her husband was a simple person employed as a low-paid *chowkidar* in the local intermediate college. She used to do sweeping work in some houses to augment the income. Thus, she was somehow managing the house. But that too appeared to be too much to the maker of her destiny.

One evening her husband came home with an unknown young man. Both looked drunk. Her husband told that the young man had recently got sweeper's job in the college. He also asked her to prepare meal for both because that man would also take dinner there. This man was very talkative and appeared to be cunning also. He was trying to get chummy with both of them. Soon her suspicion turned into reality as her husband's coming home drunk became a routine. Her husband also started gambling and losing money in it. The more he lost, the more he drank; and the more he drank, the more he lost. To clear the losses, first he sold her trinkets and then even the household utensils. It became impossible for her to feed the children and she often had to remain hungry, but the demands of her husband for money kept on increasing mercilessly. Her future and that of her sons appeared to have become totally dark. During the previous night, he brought the son of local headman with him, sent the drunken bully in her room and locked it from outside. She resisted but could not save the last thing left with her – her honor. She felt abysmally humiliated and dejected about her future. Her parents had already died and she had no other place for shelter. In a state of utter helplessness, in the early hours of morning she quietly took the two sleeping sons in her lap, came at the bridge of river Kuano and jumped into it from the bridge. When she regained her consciousness, she found some fishermen and policemen surrounding her.

Having told that she started crying pitifully, "My sons are gone. For whom shall I live? Please let me die."

According to the Indian Penal Code, Bhagwanti was guilty of double murder as well as attempt to commit suicide and her offence was punishable with death. The humane Inspector was in a great dilemma whether he should charge Bhagwanti of these crimes or not, and so he had brought her to me for guidance.

On hearing Bhagwanti's story, I was triply confounded—whether the society that could not provide her enough to feed herself and her children had any right to put her to death at the gallows, whether she was guilty for her crimes or her husband was guilty who brought those circumstances which forced her to take the extreme step, and whether the fishermen had done any favor to Bhagwanti by saving her from drowning and putting her back to a life of misery, shame and humiliation.

Anyways, I told the Inspector to write in the general diary that Bhagwanti had come to Kuano with her two sons for bathing in the river where she slipped along with the children. A fisherman, who saw her slipping, saved her from drowning but failed to save the two children.

I do not know that by doing this I gave a better future to Bhagwanti than what she would have got by being hanged.

□

# Secret of Magisterial, Judicial and Commission of Enquiry

On 16th July, 1957, when for the first time I entered B.Sc. (1st year) Statistics class, Dr. Adhikari, the professor, had started thus,

"Feel proud that you are in the elite class of Statistics (during those days, Statistics was considered toughest and hence elite). But remember that there are lies, white lies and then Statistics."

Students, who had come from Convent background understood the meaning of the wisecrack and had a hearty laugh, and *Desi* students like me, who did not understand either head or tail of this, also followed suit in order to escape looking too *Desi.*

Later, when I joined district Jhansi as A.S.P., Mr. Goel, an extremely pragmatic and successful S.P., had advised me in a similar vein,

"You know why police is so unpopular as compared to other departments? Because every other department gives something to citizens – teacher gives education, doctor gives health, engineer gives roads, and I.A.S. gives *anudan.* The policeman does not give anything: he only takes liberty. If a policeman gives something, it is either *lathi* or *goli.* Moreover, the bribe in other departments is usually a shared booty of government funds, which enriches the giver and taker both, while policeman's bribe is of personal money which pinches the giver. So the public is generally hostile to police and sees every action of a police officer, howsoever well intentioned, with suspicion. Therefore, quite often you may find yourself or your subordinates in the dock despite acting with the best of intentions. Unfortunately, situations created due to distrust often become serious or even violent without giving opportunity for persuasion or clarification. Such situations can rarely be handled by sticking to rules and laws. So, do not always be a stickler to the rules. If you do not know tricks of the trade, you may get yourself or your subordinates in trouble for none of your faults. If you or your subordinates have acted in good faith, try to save yourselves and your subordinates by all the available means.

The government is well aware of these facts. Therefore, in order to defuse such situations, it has created certain instruments called enquiries – Magisterial Enquiry, Judicial Enquiry and Commission of Enquiry. Remember that the more bombastic the name of an enquiry, the more likely it is that its report would be of no consequence. In their effect, if not in content, the reports of these enquiries rank successively in the order of lies, white lies and Statistics. So, learn to cool a hot situation by recommending one of such enquiries. If the circumstances are such that comparatively quick conclusion of enquiry is called for, then recommend Magisterial Enquiry; but, in this there will be some risk of adverse report against police. If you do not mind continuation of enquiry for 4-5 years but are more keen that everybody should escape punishment, then recommend Judicial Enquiry. And if you want to be absolutely certain of no punishment to anybody but do not mind the continuance of enquiry for decades, then recommend Commission of Enquiry."

I could not control appearance of a broad smile on my face while I was trying to assimilate the true meaning of his words. The S.P., who was looking at me intently to see that I were not taking his advice as a joke, added,

"Of course, there are also other instruments like judicial trial, C.I.D. enquiry, etc. to save the accused. In certain type of situations, they are very effective to save even the ill-intentioned government servants from punishment."

These observations of the S.P. appeared more as a rhetoric than truth to me, because they were exactly opposite of public perception. But as I grew in the administration, I realized that the S.P. had only revealed the truth quite truthfully.

The first corroboration of S.P.'s advice came when I was S.P. Pilibhit. On hearing the complaint of a village woman that not only her complaint of theft had not been written at the police station, but the Sub-Inspector had also misbehaved with her, I ordered a Dy. S.P. to conduct a quick preliminary enquiry so that exemplary punishment could be awarded to the guilty. I had assured the woman that the erring official would be dealt with severely. On the seventh day when I called the enquiring officer to know about the enquiry's progress, he dropped a surprise bomb on me,

"Sir, the enquiry had to be stopped because on the same facts, the Sub-Inspector has managed to get a criminal case u/s 354 I.P.C. (violating modesty of a woman) filed against himself in the court of judicial magistrate and the obliging magistrate has taken cognizance of it. And according to police regulations (prevailing in nineteen seventy), if a cognizable offence is made out against a policeman, a departmental enquiry on the same facts can be conducted only after conclusion of court trial. The British had incorporated this rule in police regulations to ensure that guilty police officers do not escape jail after committing cognizable offence. But after independence judicial trials got so delayed and became so maneuverable that honorable acquittal (after which departmental action also becomes barred) of accused officers has become a near certainty. Therefore, guilty officers sometimes get cases filed against themselves to take advantage of this provision."

I was furious for my inability to punish the guilty and remained tense for more than a week, but I had to remain content with simply transferring the Sub-Inspector to an insignificant post.

During the British period and for more than a decade thereafter, the C.I.D. enjoyed such a high reputation for efficiency and integrity that everybody dissatisfied with investigation by local police requested for a C.I.D. investigation. But our *Netas* soon managed to ensure that C.I.D. became so ineffective and so biased that demand for transferring investigation from district police to C.I.D. started coming from the guilty accused persons rather than from the complainant. This maneuverability of C.I.D. became clear to me when during my posting as S.P. Basti, a truck driver was badly thrashed by the son of an M.L.A. for delay in giving pass to his car. The M.L.A. was close to the C.M. I ordered arrest of the accused, but the S.O. did not muster courage and came out with an excuse that the accused had fled to Nepal. The opposition was crying foul and the matter was taking serious political overtones. Then a senior police officer close to C.M. advised me to send a request for transferring the investigation to C.I.D. on the ground of its being politically important. I did the same and the case was transferred to C.I.D. promptly. The investigating officer of C.I.D. happened to be a man with some guts. He issued a warrant of arrest of the accused. Before this warrant could be executed, this officer was transferred and another 'suitable' officer was posted in his place. He withdrew the warrant and started reinvestigation of the case. This 'suitable' officer took 'suitably long' time in investigation and ultimately gave a 'suitable' report that no arrest is called for because no independent witness had corroborated the allegation.

Magisterial enquiry is mandatory in case of firing by police. But in other cases also in which public is agitated about any police action or inaction, it is often used as an instrument of placating the public. The executive magistrates take fairly long time in completing the enquiry, which pacifies the forgetful public. Moreover, on conclusion of magisterial enquiry, any departmental or judicial action can be taken only after a senior police officer carries out departmental proceedings or registers a criminal case and investigates. It is interesting to know that British people created no such institution of executive magistrates in their own country (Britain), where the police was made directly responsible for its acts – bad or good. But in countries under British rule, this institution was created by the British to act as a buffer between the police and the public.

Judicial enquiries are ordered in matters of greater importance and have often been found of lesser value in punishing the guilty officers. My posting in Basti gave me opportunity of facing two judicial enquiries—one against myself and another against a Station Officer. They were a great eye-opener to me.

The facts in the first case were that I had got a case of cheating and misappropriation of funds registered against Mr. Pande, a ruling Congress Party M.L.A. and his shadow (a police constable) after collecting foolproof written evidence against them. On coming to know of this, the M.L.A. sent a telegram to the C.M., Speaker and I.G. (head of state police) that I had attempted to commit his murder by firing at him when he was moving in his constituency on a bicycle (during those days, M.L.A. moving on a bicycle was not the eighth wonder of the world). Next day in the Vidhan Sabha, he narrated the so-called murder attempt with eyes full of tears. As the matter related to an M.L.A.'s security and dignity the entire House got up and in unison demanded my arrest. The I.G. rang me up to know the facts. Luckily for me at the time of reported murder attempt I was at the house of a local minister, whose *Bhabhi* had died that very day. I told the I.G. accordingly and he communicated the same to the C.M. But the M.L.A.s – particularly belonging to opposition – insisted on a high-level enquiry and did not allow the House to carry on business. Then to placate them, the C.M. ordered a judicial enquiry. The judge took a long time in completing the enquiry, where I had to appear repeatedly to defend myself along with an advocate. At long last, the judge gave the true report that the allegation was false, concocted and with a motive of getting the S.P., who had registered criminal case against the M.L.A., punished. This report of the judicial enquiry was probably not read even by a *Babu* of the secretariat because no action was initiated against the M.L.A. The criminal case registered by me against the M.L.A. and his shadow was investigated by the C.I.D., which submitted charge-sheet against them (it may or may not be a coincidence that the charge-sheet was submitted after the M.L.A. was defeated in the election). But when the trial commenced, he had again become M.L.A. of the ruling Janata Dal. The trial was about to result in his conviction, when the M.L.A. got the case withdrawn by order of Mr. Banarasi Das, the then C.M.

The obliging C.M. not only withdrew the case but also made this M.L.A. a minister. And then this minister got his shadow promoted soon to the rank of Head Constable. This incident made me wise about two golden rules: First, unless a police officer has masochistic tendency of enjoying one's own discomfiture, one should not indulge in the totally futile attempt to get a politician punished for his crimes. Second, proximity to a maneuvering politician is the surest way to promotion irrespective of one's deeds.

I had to face the second judicial enquiry in a case in which Station Officer of Police Station, Dudhara, district Basti, on receiving information of communal tension due to cow slaughter in a village, had badly thrashed some Muslims of the village which was notorious for cow slaughter. Cow slaughter, being a communally sensitive matter, the incident had assumed considerable political importance not only locally but also in Lucknow. Local M.L.A., who was a Muslim, was leading the Muslim group which demanded severe action against the S.O. I had transferred the S.O. to another Police Station and asked the Circle Officer to conduct preliminary enquiry into allegations of excessive beating, so that further action could be taken (a preliminary enquiry is mandatory before commencing departmental action). But the Muslims were not satisfied, so the government ordered a judicial enquiry. A retired judge of the High Court started the enquiry and after about four years submitted a report which appeared simply amazing. The main recommendations of the report were,

1. Due to cow slaughter, a serious communal situation had developed and the S.O. had handled it very wisely by applying necessary force.
2. For having acted so wisely, the S.O. should not

only be awarded but also be promoted.

The moral of this story for me was that if a police officer wanted accelerated promotion, he should create a situation culminating in a judicial enquiry against himself.

Commissions of enquiry consist of members, who are mostly persons retired from very senior posts. They are too well aware of the fruitlessness of their report to take their work seriously. Their primary aim wisely remains to procrastinate the enquiry so as to ensure continuance of the pay and perks enjoyed by them. During my police career, I read reports of umpteen number of commissions and also about the disdain with which they were treated by the government. I also got an opportunity of facing National Police Commission, whose recommendations made in 1981 are awaiting implementation even after passage of 35 long years despite Hon'ble Supreme Court's order to implement them without delay. Thus, I can say with confidence that in case of allegations against someone, if one manages to get a Commission of Enquiry set up against oneself, then one would be safe for at least 35 years (1981-2015), which period is enough for retirement from service, if not from life.

□

# *Bina Padha-Likha Bhoot* (An Illiterate Ghost)

"Sir! Would you like meeting Baherhi Ke *Mian Jee*?" the Station Officer of Baherhi Police Station had asked me.

I was posted as S.S.P., Bareilly and had come to Baherhi from Bareilly to inspect Police Station, Baherhi. My wife Neerja and sons, Rajarshi and Devarshi, had also accompanied me. We were staying in P.W.D. inspection house. I had returned to the inspection house from the police station at about 6 p.m. and I had nothing special to do in the evening.

On my showing ignorance about *Mian Jee,* the S.O. told,

"Sir, he lives in a village a few miles away from Baherhi. He has acquired such a reputation for curing every ailment through exorcising of evil spirits from the body that his village has turned into a veritable *Mela*-ground. Hordes of villagers from distant places come to get cured daily and wait for days to get his blessings. I have met the patients vouching that they have themselves heard the howling of evil spirits invoked by *Mian Jee* during exorcising."

I thought that it would be a good fun for the family and we all started for the *Mian Jee's* village.

As we approached the village, we saw scores of bullock carts parked here and there, hundreds of patients and their attendants sitting here and there, women cooking food on ready-made hearths, and babies sleeping on ready-made beds on the bullock carts or on the ground. The S.O. had already informed the *Mian Jee* about our arrival. He received us cordially in his *baithak* and offered tea. During our tea taking, he told us that this world is full of evil spirits which are 52 times of human population in this world. I was quite amused by the certainty which *Mian Jee* displayed about the count of evil spirits, but feigned to listen to him in awe. On presuming that a great impression he had made on me, he further added,

"These *Jinnaat* (evil spirits) keep on hovering in the atmosphere around us and enter our bodies whenever opportunity (like opening your mouth for yawning) arises. Then they cause all sort of physical and mental ailments in our body; and they are the sole cause of all our troubles. If they are forced out of our bodies, we can get rid of all the ailments. I exorcise the patients of all these evil spirits. I shall show you how these *Jinnat* are made to leave the patient's body."

When it had become completely dark, we were taken to the side room which was less than 10 feet wide and 20 feet long. It had no window and had only one entrance door. Visibly, there was nothing in the room except a circle drawn at the center. A *chatai* was laid along the 10 feet long wall for us to sit. Then *Mian Jee* drew a line (*Lakshman Rekha*) in front of us and told us not to cross this line during the proceedings lest an evil spirit enter our body. Then a patient was called and asked to sit in the circle drawn at the center of the room. *Mian Jee* sat by the wall opposite to ours and an assistant came with a glass half full of water in which *Mian Jee* blew air from his mouth and then the patient was asked to drink it. Thereafter, the assistant closed the only door of the room, making it pitch dark and *Mian Jee* asked the patient to burp with all his might so that the ghost inside him comes out of his body. The patient burped a few times and then an eerie roaring voice filled the room. To us this appeared to emanate from the patient's mouth. Despite my being a non-believer in any kind of supernatural existence, a chill went through my spine. Then *Mian Jee* spoke in a commanding tone,

"Who are you and where have you come from?"

There was no reply excepting a scornful 'huh'. At this insubordination of the spirit, irate *Mian Jee* shouted,

"*Sale batata hai ki lagaun kodhe?*'

There was a sound of a stick hitting somebody's back, and then the *bhoot* capitulated,

"I am the ghost of Ram Shankar who had died of a road accident in Barabanki and I live on a banyan tree near Satrikh-Naka", came the reply in a weird sounding voice.

"I command you to leave this man forever, failing which you will have to face severe consequences. Will you obey?" *Mian Jee* threatened the spirit.

The ghost roared again and said, "Huh! You do not have enough power to make me leave his body."

*Mian Jee*'s angry response came,

"Then suffer. Go and strike your head hard with the ceiling."

And it seemed that despite protestations of the ghost, he had been lifted to the ceiling, with which his head struck and then the thud of his falling on the floor was heard. The ghost started begging for pardon and as *Mian Jee* agreed to pardon him only if he left the patient's body, he agreed to leave the patient's body forever. Then the door of the room opened and the patient left the room happily.

Next a woman patient was called in the room. From her body came out only a *shaya*, which *Mian Jee* described as a nascent ghost, and on *Mian Jee*'s command it left meekly.

Again a male patient was called from whose body came out a frighteningly roaring ghost. *Mian Jee* calmly asked,

"Where are you from?"

"I am from Allahabad and I live in a cemetery there."

"Why did you enter his body?"

"Because he had defecated on my tomb in the cemetery."

Then *Mian Jee* interrupted his conversation with the ghost and told me that if I had any question in my mind, I could ask from the ghost. I was not prepared for this, but at the spur of the moment, I got a flash in my mind to test the G.K. of the ghost, and asked,

"What is the distance from Bareilly to Moscow?"

For a few moments there was total silence and then, instead of the ghost, *Mian Jee* broke that silence,

"*Sir! yeh to bina parha-likha bhoot hai. Parha-likha aaye tab yeh sawal puchhiyega.* (Sir! This is an illiterate ghost. You should ask that question when an educated ghost appears."

□

# *Teen Tabarra-Madhe Sahiba, Machchar-Khatmal, Tikona-Samosa*

I was never a scholar of Islamic religion and knew little to differentiate between a Shia and a Sunni until I was posted as S.S.P., Lucknow in March 1980. I had taken charge as S.S.P., Lucknow in the forenoon and after meeting the staff posted in the office, I had proceeded to call on Mr. R.D. Pande, D.I.G., Lucknow Range. He was a very sober, understanding and affectionate person. After preliminaries and some wise words about the importance and necessity of remaining politically updated, he added with a grave voice,

"The adherents of Shia and Sunni sects in Lucknow are always at daggers drawn and one of the most important jobs of the police here is avoidance of Shia-Sunni riots. These riots can trigger at any time in any area having mixed population of Shias and Sunnis, and for any reasonable or unreasonable reason. So, you should make yourself fully aware of the history, extent, causes and involvement of some clerics and society leaders in these riots."

For his advice on Shia-Sunni riots, I always feel indebted to the D.I.G. because the wise words of him made me become wiser about Islam and also about the long history of Shia-Sunni riots in Lucknow. At the time of Mohammad Sahab's death, a question arose as to who should succeed him to rule the Caliphate.

Mohammad Sahab's followers got divided in two groups – one which supported the view that his closest disciple should take over the reins and the other group wanted his son-in-law Ali to take over. The first group prevailed and first Abu Bakr, then Umar and then Usman became the Caliphs. It was only after the passing away of these three Caliphs that Ali could become the Caliph. The first group that holds all the four Caliphs in high esteem is called Sunni. The second group that calls the first three Caliphs as usurpers of the throne is called Shia.

Historically, serious disputes existed between Shia and Sunni communities of Lucknow. The Moghals, who ruled the country from Delhi, were Sunni Muslims while the Nawabs of Lucknow who ruled Avadh as a protégée of the Moghals were Shias. The two rulers lived in apparent harmony, but the Shias and Sunnis of Lucknow never lived in harmony, because Sunnis, who were poorer, were derisively looked down upon by Shia Nawabs. Shia rulers allowed only limited religious activity to Sunnis. According to police records, the Shias had been traditionally taking out a whopping number of 772 religious processions—small and big—during a year in Lucknow, the Sunnis were allowed only one major procession of Moharram. After attainment of independence by the country, Sunnis speedily outgrew the Shias in economic and political power. Then they started demanding more processions for themselves and curtailment of processions of Shias. The main plea of the Sunnis for reduction of Shia processions was that the Shias in their congregations used to recite Tabarra (*Lanat* or condemnation) against the three so-called usurper Caliphs. The Shias insisted on taking out their traditional processions and not allowing any fresh processions to Sunnis, which position the police had to endorse under rules. In all cases where there is dispute between two or more groups about some religious procession, police is expected to follow the rule of adhering to tradition. So the hotter elements among Sunnis started taking out unauthorized processions and reciting Madhe-Sahiba (praise) of all Caliphs including the three Caliphs considered usurpers by Shias. In fact, the *Maulavis* of the two sects incited the youngsters among Shias to recite *Tabarra* and among Sunnis to recite *Madhe-Sahiba* as a religious duty. The recitation of *Tabarra* within hearing of Sunnis or of *Madhe-Sahiba* within hearing of Shias instantaneously turned the processions into battlefields and led to *chhurebazi, aghzani,* and bomb hurling in each others' houses.

Police had to be extremely alert at all points of the processions and in all congregations because enjoying the anonymity of a crowd it was not difficult for a Shia to quietly utter the words *Teen-Tabarra* or for a Sunni to utter *Madhe-Sahiba* within the hearing of some member of the other community. So the police had to be deployed in plain clothes also to take care of such mischief makers.

Then after some time police noticed to their bewilderment that nobody in a procession or a gathering uttered either of the two words, yet rioting, started for reasons not understood. Therefore intelligence agencies were detailed to find the cause. What they reported was an enlightening example of ingenuity of mischief makers; in fact, since then, I have become convinced that the mischief-makers possess a more fertile brain than that of a peace-loving person. Since the police used to pounce upon anybody uttering the words *Teen-Tabarra* or *Madhe-Sahiba,* the youngsters of the two sides had devised new terms to insult each other: Shias had now started calling Sunnis as *Machchar* (mosquito) and Sunnis had retaliated by calling Shias as *Khatmal* (blood-sucking bug). These words quietly uttered by some mischief monger of one community for the 'benefit' of the other community had now become a fuse for the riot-dynamite. Naturally, now the police started taking into preventive custody anybody uttering these words in presence of members of the other community. And as the bacteria mutate to develop resistance against new antibiotics, soon the Shias came out with another innovation *Tikona* (indicating the three 'usurper caliphs'). Now *Tikona* became the 'fuse-word' for the riots. When this too became known to police they came up with another epithet '*samosa*' (not the least for its deliciousness but for its three corners); and this they would utter in Lucknowi style to their buddy '*Yaar, aao chalo Samosa kha aayen* (Friend! Come let us go to eat *Samosa*)' in order to ignite the fuse.

Since the funds received clandestinely by Shia leaders from Iran and by Sunni leaders from Saudi Arabia were proportionate to the stories of atrocities committed on Shias and Sunnis respectively, no community leader was genuinely interested in containing the riots. Hence, all police efforts to control the riots went in vain and the two sides kept on inventing new excuses and new vocabulary for perpetuation of riots.

Ultimately, the government banned all processions of both the communities and then Lucknow turned into a riot-free city; of course, to the detriment of adding new words in Lucknowi lexicon.

□

# A Dwarf in One's Own Eyes

Her name was Dulari but she was a Bilaspuri; a Dulari hailing from Bilaspur does not remain a *dulari*. *Dulari* literally means a woman who is loved by all, but if she is a Bilaspuri, then her mother, father, brother, sister, husband, son, daughter, friends none have any time to express their love towards her. Immediately after getting up in the mornings, they become busy working with bricks, mortar, sand, cement and steel and continue like machines till dusk. Thereafter, the women and girls cook food and eat only after feeding the menfolk. By this time their body and soul both get so tired that no energy or inclination is left for giving or receiving love.

Dulari was one of those twenty Bilaspuris whom the labour-contractor had brought from Bilaspur and had put them at the site of my house under construction. Among those twenty Bilaspuris there were 10 men, five women, four children and Dulari. If you have ever got a house constructed then you would know that Bilaspuris are not ordinary human beings, they are robot-beings. They dig the ground like robots, make mortar like robots, carry bricks like robots, pull ground-water by hand-pumps like robots, eat like robots and during work speak only when it is essential for their work. Like Arjun they remain focused on their work alone. They can be seen smiling or sulking only when something connected with their work creates such a situation. Like robots their eyes remain full of such abject helplessness that no other emotion ever becomes visible in them. Like other Bilaspuris, Dulari also never spoke or smiled until it became unavoidable, but there was something in her big black eyes which expressed everything without her tongue uttering a word. The expression of permanent helplessness had not yet entered her eyes.

None of us knew that among those twenty Bilaspuris who was whose grandpa-grandson, wife-husband, father-son, uncle-nephew, brother-sister, friend-foe, etc. Even the contractor who had brought them had not bothered to go into such 'unnecessary' details. However, everybody had soon come to know that the name of the one with piercing looks was Dulari and she was the wife of one Robot named Laukus. This fact of her marriage had become public so soon because of the bulge of her stomach on otherwise a slim and very shapely body. I had often noticed the contractor gazing at the lifted breasts of the women climbing the stairs with bricks or mortar as head-load and he was the one who had told me about Dulari being the wife of Laukus and being pregnant.

One day out of curiosity, I had asked the contractor about the rate at which he had brought these Bilaspuris. The contractor had replied that the grown ups were at the rate of rupees two hundred, i.e. about four dollars a day and the children were at the rate of rupees one hundred fifty, i.e. about three dollars a day. Then in a conspiratorial tone, he had added,

"Although Dulari is incapable of lifting heavy loads, yet I pay her full two hundred rupees a day."

For such a hard work, this rate was too low and I had told the contractor, "You have brought them too cheap." The contractor had replied with a smile,

"In the dry region of Bilaspur, hardly anything grows and moreover this is a drought year. If I don't provide them work, they will starve...."

The contractor was saying all this with pride of a cunning tradesman, but I was feeling sorry at the plight of these hapless laborers. As the contractor's blurting of his exploits became intolerable, I interjected,

"But is it possible to even feed the family properly at this rate?"

I was unaware that Dulari was listening to our conversation. Suddenly, I looked back and found her looking straight at my eyes as if she was trying to fathom my heart and read that my words had any real sympathy for them or were mere impotent fulminations. I felt that my persona had become an open book before her and in that she had read that my words were hollow and there was no ability or irrepressible desire to do something for them. Then Dulari turned her eyes off me and quietly got engaged in her work as if nothing had happened in between, but I felt that in the short duration of those moments, Dulari had made me a dwarf in my own eyes.

Thereafter, one morning when I went there, I found that no laborer had come to work. The contractor informed me,

"Today the labor will come two hours late as they have gone for the cremation of Dulari's still-born baby. Yesterday while climbing the staircase, she had got a jerk in her stomach and had aborted during the night."

On hearing this, I got so upset that I left the site immediately. After a week when I came back to the site, I was surprised to see that Dulari was as usual mixing cement with sand. On seeing me she only momentarily raised her eyebrows and then immediately became engrossed in preparing the mortar. I knew that in her heart, a storm of sorrow was blowing but there was no trace of tears in her eyes. Despite a strong desire to express my condolences, I could not speak a word to her. Instead, I took the contractor aside and asked him,

"After the abortion, why has she come to work so soon?" The contractor looked at me askance and said,

"Then what will she eat? She has also to repay me rupees one hundred which her husband had taken as advance from me to meet the expenses of cremation of the still-born baby."

By the end of the month of February, the structure of the house had been raised and the walls had been plastered. Now the plumber and the carpenter had started working on it. One day the contractor had not come. Sitting on a rickety chair, I was looking into the book of accounts, when Laukus came to me and told hesitatingly,

"*Sahab*! The contractor has not given the last month's wages to any of us. He was saying that you have not yet made payment to him for the work done last month."

On my assurance that I had already made up-to-date payment to the contractor, Laukus' face turned yellow as if the blood had been drained out of it. On regaining composure and after gathering some courage, he spoke,

"*Sahab*, then I think we are being duped in the same way as a contractor had done with us in Delhi two years back. Knowing that every year we go back home in the month of April, he had started delaying payments since the month of February. And when we had reached the state of starvation, we had left for our homes without receiving payments." Then after a pause, Laukus added beseechingly,

"*Sahab*! Kindly help us to get our dues."

I got very agitated and started thinking to do something against the contractor. Laukus' show of courage to speak against the contractor had inspired me to do something for the Bilaspuris – and particularly so because Laukus was husband of Dulari, whose looks had once dwarfed me in my own estimation. I wrote a complaint addressed to police against the contractor and got it signed by all the Bilaspuris. Then I sent a message to the contractor that if the payment to the Bilaspuris was not made by that evening, I shall get the complaint lodged at the police station. Next day on my way to the construction site, I was in a great dilemma that if the contractor had not paid the wages, then the Bilaspuris would soon leave for their homes and then how shall I pursue the long drawn and most likely a fruitless case against the contractor. But as soon as I reached the site, I found Dulari staring at me and I don't know how her eyes convincingly conveyed to me that their payment had been made. I felt that I was not so dwarf as I had thought myself to be; and the comprehension that Dulari's eyes were also conveying the same message elevated my spirit immensely.

But this feeling of heightened self-esteem could not last long because after a few days only, when I reached the construction site, I did not find Dulari and Laukus there. When I asked the contractor about them, he casually replied,

"Since the time of miscarriage, Dulari had started shirking the work; therefore, I have fired her and Laukus."

This reply hardly convinced me because I had never found Dulari shirking her work – not even during those moments when with the piercing looks of her big eyes, she used to decipher truth and falsehood, sin and sacredness, ill-will and goodness, selfishness and altruism in other person's heart; and within a few days, I could know through gossip that one day when

Dulari was working alone in the bathroom, the contractor had made an attempt to violate her modesty. For fear of losing her honor in the society, she had not complained to anybody but had left the work here.

Then one day when I was going to the market, I saw Dulari working at the site of a road under repair. She raised her eyebrows and her eyes met mine. She kept on looking at me for a few moments without a wink. In those eyes, I saw that she was clearly seeing that despite my desire to avenge her dishonor, I had neither the ability nor the courage to do so. A guilt feeling arose like a lump in my heart that I was not only incapable of avenging the injustice done to her but was also indirectly a party to it.

Again I started looking like a dwarf in my own eyes.

□

# Dewedy! You Have Burnt Your Boat

The day had been rather hot and so was the emergency general meeting of the I.P.S. Association being held in the police officers' mess in Lucknow. The issue was arbitrary suspension of S.P. Unnao by the Chief Minister. I, being the President of the Association, was calmly receiving the fumes and flames emanating from the mouth of speaker after speaker.

I.P.S. officers are officially permitted to form an association, but the rules specifically prohibit the association from taking up, discussing or agitating any cause of individual officers. It has a limited role of presenting before the D.G. Police and the government issues of general interest of I.P.S. officers and of police administration. These issues often relate to the pay, promotion and privileges of I.P.S. officers or their power in enforcing law and order. In fact, I.P.S. Association serves little purpose other than providing an opportunity to younger officers to rave and rant in its meetings – often held only once in a year – about failure of its executive in achieving anything concrete for the officers during the bygone year. Even if a Chief Minister agrees to some proposal of the association, the I.A.S. officers sitting in the secretariat start maneuvering things in such a way that the matter does not reach the C.M. in the form of a formal proposal on a file. Any increase in the pay, privileges or powers of I.P.S. officers is seen by I.A.S. officers as a relative reduction in their own pay, privileges and powers. So as soon as a file relating to any of these subjects is put up before the I.A.S. officers, they become rattled like a bull being shown a red rag. And they try to scuttle the proposal by hook or by crook and often the file is deliberately got misplaced in the labyrinth of the secretariat. A glaring example of this is that once an order was issued by the government to introduce Police Commissioner system in Kanpur. Mr. V.S. Panjani, I.P.S. was nominated to take charge as the first Police Commissioner of Kanpur. Losing no time, the top I.A.S. coterie met the C.M. same evening and was successful in persuading him to send Mr. Panjani to Bombay and Bangalore for two weeks to learn functioning of the Police Commissioner system there. This period of two weeks was long enough for the I.A.S. officers to win over a large number of powerful ministers and M.L.As. who started vociferously calling the introduction of Police Commissioner system as the establishment of Police-Raj in the state. And the I.A.S. officers had the last laugh because by the time Mr. Panjani returned, the C.M. had already withdrawn the order of introduction of the Police Commissioner system in Kanpur. I had the unique opportunity of serving this toothless body as Hony. Secretary for four years, and then as President for three years. This was not because I had any special qualification for heading toothless bodies; actually, I was repeatedly elected as Hony. Secretary because many members thought that I might possibly jump where the devils would not dare to tread. And I can proudly boast of an achievement which all my predecessors had failed to achieve: I got the D.I.G. placed above the district magistrate in the order of precedence. So far as my remaining President of the Association for three long years is concerned, it was merely because of a tradition in the Association that only the senior-most I.P.S. officer (excluding the D.G. Police) was unanimously elected as its president. When I became senior-most I.P.S. officer of the state, I was thrice bypassed for the post of D.G. Police by my more 'resourceful' juniors, and, therefore, thrice I became the President of the Association.

This emergency meeting was being held during my last tenure as President of the Association. A ruling party leader had alleged that the S.P., Unnao had misbehaved with him and the S.P. was placed under suspension. The truth was that this leader had himself rubbed the S.P. on the wrong side and the S.P. had retorted befittingly. I.P.S. officers, on knowing about this unjust suspension, got very agitated and an emergency meeting of the Association was called in the evening in Police Officers' Mess. In this meeting, a resolution was passed that the entire house would immediately proceed to the C.M.'s residence and demand revocation of unfair suspension. And accordingly, we reached 5, Kalidas Marg (C.M.'s residence) at about 11 p.m. after informing his secretary. After making us wait for quite some time, Mr. Ram Prakash, C.M. came to the meeting room and, before listening to us, expressed his displeasure on our having barged in without prior appointment. However, on our telling him that the entire I.P.S. cadre was feeling extremely demoralized on the suspension of the S.P. because the B.J.P. leader himself had given cause for the treatment meted out to him, he mellowed down a bit and told (although grudgingly) that he will look into the matter. Next morning when I woke up, I was happy to read the headline on the first page of all the newspapers – "Revocation of suspension of S.P. Unnao under I.P.S. Association's pressure."

I knew that the revocation of suspension had happened mainly because the Chief Minister Mr. Ram

Prakash was a very sensible person. More than that, I realized that Mr. Ram Prakash was a thorough gentleman because I had led the agitation for a cause of an individual officer which was not within the purview of the Association's functions and was unprecedented; and as per rules, I could myself have been placed under suspension for having done that. I had become sure of one thing that after this incident, no Chief Minister would ever dream of appointing me as D.G. Police. This belief was reinforced when one day I happened to meet Mr. J.N. Chaturvedi, retired D.G. Police, who had a liking for me. He consolingly told me, 'Dewedy! You have burnt your boat.'

And lo and behold! It was Mr. Ram Prakash himself, who appointed me D.G. Police, U.P. when the then incumbent retired.

□

# The *Rosogulla* Service

Inaugural addresses and valedictory addresses must contain pep-talk. So, Mr. Dutt, I.C.S., Director, National Academy of Administration, Mussoorie, had started his valedictory address thus,

"You all have been selected through the same competitive examination, are members of class one services and have undergone Foundational Course here together in a spirit of camaraderie. In future, you are going to face the highest responsibilities individually and jointly. Therefore, always remember to work with a spirit of fraternity and equality."

However, after working in the field, we soon learnt that there was a hidden catch in the word 'jointly' spoken by Mr. Dutt. In fact, there was hardly any position of real authority where I, as a police officer, could take important decisions without supervisory interference by some I.A.S. officer either as D.M./ Commissioner or as Home Secretary/Chief Secretary or both. Top officers of other departments were also compelled to take decisions 'jointly', where the I.A.S. – Secretary had the upper hand. We also learnt that fraternity may be kept at personal level, but in office, equality is possible only among equals.

The I.A.S., essentially, has only the land-revenue collection department under it but, in effect, the I.A.S. is a *Rosogulla* service. *Rosogulla* can be smoothly downed through one's esophagus even in an otherwise full stomach. Similarly, the I.A.S. manages to enter with *Rasgulla*-like smoothness the top echelons of any department and grab its control. It creates space for itself. The I.A.S., which is as smooth as a *Rosogulla* in its movements, is like an octopus in spreading its tentacles to search space at the top of any department or organization and then spread its tentacles there. The I.A.S. dominates all other services in the capacity of District Magistrates in the field and as secretaries in the government. They also keep a vigilant eye for any opportunity to enter a key position in other departments and organizations. Earlier there used to be no place for I.A.S. in Medical Department, in Electricity Board, in Council of Scientific and Industrial Research, etc. but the I.A.S. slowly but steadily managed to enter there in the guise of Director Administration (in medical department), Joint Secretary, Administration (in C.S.I.R.), Chairman and M.D. in State Electricity Board, etc. This helps them not only to twist the tail of other departments, but also to expand their cadre to ensure early promotions. During nineteen sixties when I had joined the service, a new entrant to I.A.S. took 23-24 years to become a Commissioner. Now this duration has been reduced to 13-14 years in many states.

So far as the growth of I.C.S. was concerned, the British kept a tight leash, because they preferred efficient administration to fatter administrative services. The Chief Secretary, Chairman Board of Revenue, and the I.G. Police, who were highest functionaries of the state, were all in the rank of Joint Secretary to the Government of India. After independence, its successor I.A.S. cadre was itching to ensure quicker promotions for itself. So, they persuaded the politicians to create umpteen number of new departments and corporations in the government headed by I.A.S. officers. The number of secretaries also started multiplying accordingly. In the year 1970, I was S.P. of district Pilibhit and Yogesh Chandra, a friendly person, was D.M. there. He smilingly told me one day that the post of Chief Secretary had been upgraded to that of Secretary to Govt. of India. Then a bit sullenly added, "Still it took too long for I.A.S. officers to become commissioners, but we are planning to bring down this period to 14 years." And true to his words in 1980 I.A.S. Officers of 1966 batch had been promoted as Commissioners.

Then Newton's law of inertia started applying undaunted in case of growth of top jobs—the expansion continued because there was no resisting force to stop it: the I.A.S. Officers tried to accelerate expansion and politicians acted as puppets in their hands. Before independence in the Uttar Pradesh cadre of I.A.S. there were only two posts of the rank of Joint Secretary, G.O.I. Now there are about 100 posts of this rank, about 50 posts of Addl. Secy.'s rank and about 20 posts of full Secretary's rank. Once this loot of higher posts by I.A.S. Officers started, other services felt being left behind because in comparison to I.A.S. they started losing in promotion, perks and prestige. So, a rat race for promotions in all departments commenced and in order to keep mouths of officers of other services shut, the I.A.S. officers started throwing some crumbs towards them also. On one occasion when I was talking about this gross wastage to the Principal Secretary, Home, he derisively retorted, "Why should you bother? When *Allah meharban gadaha pahalwan.*" I knew that by *Allah* here he meant 'The I.A.S.' and I did not want to think about what he meant by '*Gadaha*'.

The ability to waste government funds with impunity adds to the sense of power of the I.A.S. and our politicians being powerless to stop it, have started 'jointly' enjoying this criminal waste. The new generation Chief Ministers make almost every M.L.A. belonging to ruling group either a minister or give them some position with the status and privileges of a minister – and so there is often a *khel* minister along with a *kud* minister. Thus, the 'KHEL-KUD' of I.A.S. and politicians continues in the loot of powers, privileges and pelf.

□

# The Secret of Veiled Threats

It is a common knowledge among officers that "In the Secretariat, there is only one secret that there is no secret." The reason for this is that the power to harass each and every person that comes in their contact, enjoyed by the secretariat *Babus* (of all ranks and stature), turns most of them into megalomaniacs. Therefore, some of them must disclose in public everything, however confidential it may be, if for no other gain then just to boast of one's importance. I had the first-hand experience of it even before joining the service. After my selection into the I.P.S., I along with a friend of mine had gone to the house of a junior level assistant posted in the secretariat. The assistant was a relative of my friend, so he welcomed us into his drawing room. From his initial talks, he appeared to be a fairly normal young man, but as soon as my friend told him that I had been selected in the I.P.S., he started giving hints of the importance of his work in the secretariat. And then without anybody's asking told us that he had come home after transferring two S.Ps. on that very day. At that time, I had no idea by whom these officers were transferred and, therefore, listened to him like a dumb doll, but the claim appeared to be too big to swallow without a glitch. So, during our return journey, I disclosed my suspicions to my friend, who being more knowledgeable, told me that this fellow was doing the job of a typist in the secretariat, and today he must have typed those transfer orders which he was imagining to be his own orders.

There is one more secret of the secretariat which is little known to the public – the power of veiled threats. I do not know that the proverb that 'king can do no wrong' is based on truth or not, but I can assert with confidence that in India 'secretariat can do no wrong'. On two occasions, I had first-hand experience of this infallibility of the secretariat. For I.A.S./P.C.S. officers manning the secretariat the vehicles are provided by the secretariat administration. Since in the government order, there is no provision of vehicles for the *Mem Sahibs* (lady wives), children and pets of the secretaries (whose levels and numbers keep on swelling like mushroom every year), the secretariat keeps on snatching the vehicles of the departments and corporations supervised by them. These vehicles are commandeered unauthorized by extending veiled threats. The functioning of the reticent departments is made tough by withholding grants, delaying proposals, writing disgracefully worded letters, making secret complaints to the minister and misplacing or outrightly destroying the service records of the reticent officers. After communal riots of 1980, the Home Secretariat had managed to get a government order issued that a control room would function round the clock in the Secretariat and seven vehicles purchased for police department will be placed at the disposal of this control room for quick dispatch of orders. In 1992, when I was posted Addl. Director General, Police Headquarters, I found that instead of seven, as many as 13 vehicles of police department were attached to this control room. Since I knew that even seven vehicles were more than needed for the limited functions of the control room, I wrote a letter to the Principal

Secretary, Home to return the extra six vehicles for performing field duties. No reply was received nor was any action taken on my letter. On my orally pressing the matter with the Principal Secretary, Home, I was tersely told that if I persist an enquiry would be ordered about use of vehicles by police officers of the state. Since my D.G. was also of no help in the matter, I stopped pursuing the matter.

During this very posting of mine another case, which was a real eye opener, occurred. The Central Government had allotted a few crores of rupees for purchase of certain specified equipment for modernization of the state police. The state secretariat while releasing this grant in the month of September wrote that the Police Headquarter must utilize the entire grant before the coming 31st March and that the Police Headquarter must obtain administrative approval (from Home Secretariat) and Financial approval (from Finance Secretariat) before making any purchases. Many of these items had to be imported through the State Trading Corporation, New Delhi. Since the time was short, I put myself wholeheartedly on the job and wrote to S.T.C. for arranging purchases and to the Home Secretary for administrative as well financial approval. The S.T.C. provided us with the quotation of rates and communicated that they will proceed with the purchases only after receiving the price in advance. As no reply was received from the Home Secretariat for a long time, I sent an officer there who brought a letter stating that the administrative approval was being given for two months but no purchases should be made before financial approval is received from Finance Secretary. As per procedure, financial approval could be obtained by Home Secretary only from the finance secretariat (and not by P.H.Q. directly), so I wrote back for expeditiously sending the financial approval. After the lapse of two months I received a letter of the home secretariat conveying financial approval for a period of one month. Since the administrative approval had lapsed by now, I wrote to Home Secretary to renew it expeditiously, whose approval was received after the lapse of the financial approval. And this race continued till March, but I never received the two approvals for concurrent periods.

At the end of financial year, I felt sorry for not being able to purchase the equipment for modernization of the police, but was not feeling guilty for the same because I had left no stone unturned to perform the job. But I was shocked beyond belief when in the month of May, I received a letter from the Principal Secretary, Home conveying displeasure of the government for not utilizing the grant within the financial year and demanding explanation for the same for being put up before the Chief Minister.

By now I had learnt that whatever I write, the Chief Minister will know only what the secretariat wants him to know. So, instead of writing to the secretariat that they were exclusively responsible for whatever had happened, I sent a simple letter stating the facts. No reply was ever received to this letter.

□

# A Case for Suspension Dole to Policemen

It was already 10 a.m. and the advocate was naturally in a hurry to reach the High Court (Lucknow Bench) while being mentally engrossed in the thoughts of the arguments with which he was going to floor the prosecuting counsel. So, he 'arguably' rammed the car that he was driving into the slow-moving army truck going ahead of him. As a colleague's car was damaged near the court, it would have amounted to losing an argument, if the horde of advocates had failed to chase the army driver and attempt to lynch him. Then the 'law-knowing' advocate-fraternity did 'understandably' not tolerate the lawful intervention of policemen to save the driver from their clutches and they 'dutifully' started thrashing the policemen, blocking the traffic, and burning police vehicles, government buses, etc. And to placate the vote-worthy advocate-*samaj* the government 'wisely' ordered the suspension of sub-inspector A.K. Dwivedy and registration of a case of assault against policemen for 'unwisely' using force to save their lives from the marauding advocates. We pride ourselves in becoming *nirlipt* and *nisprah* when the occasion is to face the powerful, so the media 'conscientiously' did not bother to expose the government which had 'routinely' performed the act of suspending some police officer in order to please a vote-worthy group. Actually, we the citizens of Uttar Pradesh, should feel proud that the honorable Chief Minister had himself 'valiantly' announced this suspension through the electronic media to remove any doubts in advocates' minds about his 'fearlessness' in pleasing them.

No species on earth is so selfishly adaptable for its survival as that of politicians. If Darwin had the chance of observing this species, he need not have wasted his years in fish-stinking, mosquito-ridden, mice-infested ships observing the behavior of various species and would have come to the same conclusion of 'Survival of the Fittest' sitting in cozy comfort of his house. So once the politicians discovered its efficacy, they made policemen's suspension a regular weapon for defusing explosive situations and keeping the power-groups contented. Though no political party is totally abhorrent to using this weapon, yet every party with a '*samaj*' or '*samajvadi*' tag in its name, has dexterously mastered the art of suspensions of policemen as a placatory measure for any political or mischievous power-group. Umpteen examples exist to prove this hypothesis. In the year 1995, learned advocates of Allahabad High Court had indulged in acts of hooliganism and vandalism in the court compound – may be, "with intent to have first-hand experience of the acts of some of their unruly clients so as to be able to better prepare their defense in future." At that time the judges had left their courts – possibly to avoid becoming witnesses to learned advocates' 'not-so-learned' acts; so the advocates had 'rightly' felt ignored and in order to make their presence felt had forcibly entered the chamber of the Chief Justice. Then, in order to keep tell-tale marks of their 'valor' for his subsequent notice, they had vandalized whatever they could lay their hands upon there. On being informed of their pranks, the Chief Justice was not particularly pleased. Those who are familiar with the working of the courts know it very well that it is neither easy nor advisable for the judges to take action against the advocates; therefore, the Chief Justice wisely vented his anger against the State Government and a rumor took wings that he was going to write for dismissal of the state government for failure of law and order in the state. On hearing this the 'wrestler' C.M. got so panicky that without finding about the authority of the Chief Justice to get a government dismissed, he promptly placed the then I.G., Allahabad Zone under suspension, The 'unholy' hurry was intended to mollify the Chief Justice before he could write for dismissal of the government. This I.G., who was my junior and rather close to me, later revealed a secret to me that soon after his suspension he was called by the C.M. and was quietly handed over an envelope containing rupees four lakhs – as a compensation for bearing the suspension for a few months without murmur. I felt highly jealous of the I.G. because during nineties of the past century, Rs. four lacs was such a huge sum that I would have traded my suspension for this amount any time.

Once the politicians have discovered that policemen are 'suspendable commodity', they have started placing them under suspension for mollifying their bloated egos as well. In a 'Law and Order' meeting held at Allahabad, an I.G. was suspended by 'Dalit ki Beti' for having asked a clarification on a blatantly senseless statement of her (the C.M.). Later, when the C.M. learnt that the I.G. with a Jat-like name was in fact a Dalit himself, he was reinstated without any proceedings. During the next term of this very C.M., he was posted as D.G. Police despite being juniormost in that rank.

However, it has been seen that the climax of suspension drama often takes U-turn if the affected party possesses sufficient nuisance value. Once a Principal Secretary mustered courage to suspend two assistants posted under him in the secretariat. The secretariat employees, on whose 'mercy' the government functions and with whose collaboration ministers prosper, went on lightning strike, misbehaved with the principal secretary and *gheraoed* C.M.'s office. The 'valiant' C.M. took no time in personally announcing immediate reinstatement of the two assistants along with assurance for early transfer of the Principal Secretary.

Since it will amount to 'mad-optimism' to expect our political bosses to stop using suspension of policemen as a weapon in their game of pleasing the powerful, there is a very strong case for paying suspension-allowance (other than the half salary paid under present rules) to policemen. If the politicians fight shy of openly paying such an allowance, then they should take a cue from the 'Four-Lac-Envelope-of-Chief Minister' and keep secretly handing over such envelopes to the suspended policemen. This will make the policemen willing to accept the suspension in good humor.

□

# An Alternative Way to Become Chief Secretary

Every I.A.S. officer aspires to rise to become Chief Secretary of the state to which he is allotted. Before Mandalization of the society, it was traditional to appoint known honest and efficient officers only on this prestigious post. However, Mandalization of the society in 1991 unleashed such forces as have not only made such norms redundant but have also established totally opposite norms.

The Mandal-effect conclusively divided not only the country's politics but also the bureaucracy. This division was not limited to dalit/backward/forward caste-factions only, but also to dishonest-partisan officers who managed to become blue-eyed boys of politicians versus of-little-use-to-politicians honest officers. The establishment of supremacy of dishonesty over honesty in bureaucracy started attracting every other I.A.S. officer to greener pastures of corruption. Soon the condition became so abhorrent that some conscientious and zealot young I.A.S. officers brought out a resolution in the meeting of I.A.S. Association of U.P. that in order to put a break to this ever-increasing depravity and improve the image of the Association, there should be voting in the Association to name the most corrupt I.A.S. officers. The names of the toppers of this list should be forwarded to the government with recommendation to take punitive action against them. This move was strongly opposed and all means were applied by the corrupt officers to scuttle it, but through the dogged perseverance for about a year of those honest officers, ultimately secret voting was done and the names of three officers elected most corrupt were forwarded to the government. Although the names were not publicly declared, yet the subject had generated such interest in the media that the three names including their order of (de)merit became known the very next day. These officers already had a very bad reputation and, therefore, people were quite satisfied with the result of the voting.

Then not only the I.A.S. Association but the entire state started eagerly awaiting the reaction of the government. Initially, a few articles were seen in the press criticizing the act of such a voting in the I.A.S. Association; then there was a lull for a few days. Thereafter, to everybody's wonderment, news came that one of those three officers had been posted as Secretary to Chief Minister. Soon came the elections which brought change of ruling party in the government. Again people started expecting that now adverse action will be taken against the most corrupt officers. But to everybody's astonishment, the new Chief Minister not only kept the same officer as Secretary to the Chief Minister but also posted another officer, who headed the list of most corrupt officers, on the very important post of Agriculture Production Commissioner. And during his next tenure as Chief Minister, he elevated this officer to the all-important post of the Chief Secretary, and after attainment of retirement age by this officer, he gave him extension in service for his outstanding record (in corruption). Then somebody filed public interest litigation in the Supreme Court against such a shameless flouting of service norms and for the first time in the history of the country, honorable Court ordered this officer's removal through immediate retirement. However, this did not daunt the Chief Minister and he posted the third most corrupt I.A.S. officer in the list as Chief Secretary.

This story's moral is that saving exceptions most of the Chief Ministers – forward, backward or *dalit* – are themselves on the look out for the most corrupt I.A.S. officers to post them as their secretaries and on other top jobs. By declaring somebody as most corrupt you are only making their search for the corrupt officers easier. It is now widely believed that many an officer is eagerly waiting to be declared the Most Corrupt.

□

# The Obstacle-Creators' Club

Mr. V.S. Katara, was posted as D.M., Moradabad in 1968. He was a veteran I.A.S. officer who had worked in the U.P. Government secretariat for many years. He was a happy-go-lucky, pleasant and frank person. At that time, I was Commandant, P.A.C., Moradabad. He had invited some senior officers including myself for dinner at his residence. I was new in government job and, therefore, had not fully understood him when he had remarked,

"U.P. Government Secretariat is the biggest club of the state."

The full import of his saying had dawned on me later when I learnt that it was not only the biggest club of U.P. but also the single largest body of obstacle-creators in the path of disposal of work. Majority of the employees of the secretariat live for creating obstruction and earn by creating obstruction in disposal of somebody's work. If we compare this secretariat with a secretariat of any progressive state of the country, we shall discern an obvious difference that while U.P. secretariat employees make money by delaying decisions, the employees of progressive states like Gujarat and Maharashtra make money by expediting decisions.

There is one more unique characteristic of U.P. secretariat that the decision-making stops at the Section Officer level. Once a noting is made on a file by a Section Officer, the officers above him – Dy. Secretary, Joint Secretary, Special Secretary, Secretary, and Principal Secretary – appear to have no choice but to sign their approval; only the bravest among them occasionally differ, but that too only to the extent of asking the Section Officer to reconsider his opinion – none has been seen to outrightly override Section Officer's opinion. The working relationship between the Section Officer and Secretary can be aptly compared to that which exists between the Chief Minister and the Governor: the Governor usually signs on the dotted lines written by the Chief Minister and if he differs he can only request the Chief Minister for reconsideration. And if some I.A.S. officer with suicidal tendencies does dare to issue final order which is contrary to the opinion given by the 'venerable' Section Officer, the Section Officer often uses his prerogative of delaying the actual issuance of the order till such time as he is 'pleased' by its beneficiary.

I had the misfortune of having first-hand experience of Section Officers' authority in procrastinating decision-making on many unenviable occasions. I shall quote one incident – for the benefit of uninitiated – about the perfection of art of obstacle creation by U.P. Secretariat. During British period, department of P.W.D. (Public Works Department) was created for construction of government buildings and roads. Due to manifold development activities started after independence, it got overworked and to cope with the additional construction work, the government created Nirman Nigam, Bridge Corporation, Police Housing Corporation, Jal Nigam, etc. There was one more 'alluring' reason for creation of these corporations. These corporations provided increasing avenues of promotions to the bureaucrats and greener pastures to graze to them as well as to the *Netas*.

Therefore, so many corporations were created by the year 1990 that the P.W.D. itself became thoroughly under-worked. This created an unhealthy rat-race amongst the P.W.D. and various corporations to grab maximum possible construction works from government by hook or by crook (paying bribe to ministers and officials of the secretariat). During this period, I was posted Chairman-cum-Managing Director of Police Housing Corporation and Engineer Govind Ram was its General Manager, Technical. The government had yet not authorized any officer of the corporations to grant technical approval for construction of any work and, therefore, estimates of all works had to be sent to P.W.D. for technical approval because its officers alone were authorized to grant technical approval. In the beginning when P.W.D. was overworked, it happily gave technical approval to the estimates sent by the corporations, but when it became under-worked, it stopped giving approval to the estimates of the corporations stating that it was not their job. Even P.W.D. Secretary supported this view. The underlying idea was to make the corporations dysfunctional so that in future all works were perforce allotted to P.W.D. only. Therefore, the construction activity stopped in all corporations including mine. I as well as the Chairpersons of other corporations approached the government to authorize our G.M.s for technical approval. After our more than six months' efforts, a high level meeting was held in the secretariat in which P.W.D. came up with every sort of argument to create obstacle in authorizing the G.M.s for technical approval. Ultimately, a decision was taken that the corporations will send the bio-data of their G.Ms. to their respective secretaries in government which will decide as to which G.Ms. were competent enough to be authorized. Accordingly I wrote to the Principal

Secretary, Home that my G.M. Govind Ram had passed B.E. with distinction and also M.E. with merit and had 23 years' experience as civil engineer. I also enclosed copies of his B.E. and M.E. marks-sheets. Since my works were standstill, I kept on pursuing the matter regularly and then after full six months I received a shocking reply from the government that since I had not enclosed the copies of the marks-sheets of High School and Intermediate examinations of Govind Ram no decision could be taken. This letter was signed by a Joint Secretary (P.C.S. officer), and must have had the approval of his seniors. The internal story was that the Section officer had been 'sufficiently pleased' by the P.W.D. officers to procrastinate the decision by every possible means. Therefore, he had made this funny noting of the necessity to examine High School and Intermediate marks-sheets while deciding the capability of Er. Govind Ram, M.E. And the poor I.A.S. Secretary could not muster courage to overrule his Section Officer.

I spoke about the absurdity of this requirement with the Principal Secretary who regretfully replied that now since a letter had been issued on the file; the matter can be reconsidered only after I sent a reply. So, I sent a reply with which I enclosed not only the copies of the marks-sheets of High School and Intermediate examinations but also of eighth class. Who knows the secretariat might have asked for this next time? Since no reply was forthcoming even now, I again went to the Principal Secretary, who called for the file and made a noting on the file that Mr. Govind Ram was quite competent. But, instead of issuing the order for authorizing him for technical sanction, he made a noting that now the file should be sent to Finance Secretary for formal approval. I came back happily but heard nothing from the secretariat during the next 28 days. So, I sent an officer to finance department to find out the status of the case. The officer came back with a reply that the matter had not yet been referred by home secretariat to finance secretariat. I asked this officer to contact the Section Officer of home secretariat. He was tersely told by the Section Officer that the file could not be sent to finance secretariat due to non-availability of a *chaparasi* (person who moves files from one room to another of the secretariat and who are seen loitering aplenty in the corridors of secretariat).

To cut the long story short, it took me a year to obtain the approval resulting in equally long delay in construction of buildings and commensurate escalation of cost.

□

# Manava Kahe Guman Kare?

"It was a chilly winter evening and the house-warming party was on its peak in the newly built house of a bureaucrat. From Red Label to Green Label and from Handi-chicken to Caviar – you name a drink or a dish and it was available before you blinked the eye. And why should it not be so? – After all, the house built by the bureaucrat was a palatial one. Every one was vying with each other to congratulate the bureaucrat – more with intent to please him because of his closeness to the Chief Minister than for the grandeur of the house, which was, in fact, fuelling the fire of envy in the whiskey—hot hearts of many guests. The guests had not yet left when, in the middle of the night, the bureaucrat's mobile started filling the air with a not-too-timely note of a *Bhajan 'Manava Kahe Guman Kare'*. For the bureaucrat, who had loaded this song in the phone for creating an impression on the listeners of his being worldly-unattached, the *Bhajan* was ominous. He pressed the green button with some uncalled for trepidation, but felt relieved when the other party, who was Chief Minister's Private Secretary, told him that the C.M. wanted to see him first thing in the morning. Such calls were not infrequent for this bureaucrat and this one only further inflated his bloated ego. He took no time in letting others know that the call was from C.M.'s residence and the C.M. wanted to meet him in the morning.

Next morning as he entered the C.M.'s drawing room, she smilingly told him,

"Congratulations. I have heard about your new house and the grand house-warming party of the previous night."

And before the bureaucrat could utter 'Thank you madam' she added,

"By the way how much the house has cost you?"

Haltingly, the bureaucrat uttered, "Madam, forty lakhs", because he was in a position to explain the expenditure of forty lakhs only through all his savings and loans. The remaining one core sixty lakhs had come through what is euphemistically called *ooapri kamai*.

The smile on the Chief Minister's lips would have appeared too endearing to the bureaucrat because he could not suppress his own smile when the eyes of the two met for a moment. But the officer's smile could last only till he heard the C.M. calling her Private Secretary and ordering him to hand over a sum of rupees forty *lakhs* to the bureaucrat and asking the bureaucrat to hand over the key and papers of the house to the Private Secretary. The C.M. was magnanimous enough to explain to the officer that her brother, whose workplace was near this house, had immensely liked it. She also added smilingly, "How can a sister disregard her dear brother's wishes?"

At that very moment, the tune of the officer's phone '*Manava Kahe Guman Kare*' started ringing again.

□

# Application of Law – West vs. India

## 1. Conviction on Recovered Memories of Long Ago Abuse (in the West)

There is news for our lawmakers and courts. Many of them will be horrified to learn that on a report lodged by the victim after nearly two decades of the occurrence of the crime, a conviction has been handed out merely on the basis of the memories of the victim. I quote Associated Press of the U.S.A. thus:

"Defrocked priest Paul Shanley was convicted on Monday (7th Feb., 2005) of repeatedly raping and fondling a boy at his Roman Catholic Church during the 1980s. The victim, now 27, put his head down and sobbed as the verdicts were announced after a trial that turned on the reliability of what the man claimed were recovered memories of the long ago abuse.

During the trial, the accuser broke down on the stand as he testified in graphic detail that Shanley pulled him out of Sunday morning catechism classes and molested him in the bathroom, the rectory, the confessional and the pews starting when he was 6 and continuing for six years.

'He told me that nobody would ever believe me if I told anybody,' he testified.

The defense called just one witness – a psychologist who said that so-called recovered memories can be false, even if the accuser ardently believes they are true. A lawyer for Shanley argued that the accuser was either mistaken or concocted the story with the help of personal injury lawyers to cash in on a multimillion-dollar settlement resulting from the sex scandal."

I hope this news should make us sit and think because this is not a sentence handed out in some middle-east monarchy or a tribal community, but in one of the most modern democracies that values personal liberty. In our country, criminals are often let off the hook on such grounds as delay (only of a few days) in lodging the report of the crime, uncorroborated testimony of the victim (even if the judge believes it to be true), and failure of the prosecution to prove the case beyond reasonable doubt (even if the judge knows that this failure was occasioned by the delay in trial or extra-legal efforts of the criminal or his lawyer). Unwittingly, we value our liberty most so long as it is liberal towards the accused; the liberty of the victim is often our last concern. So why bemoan that criminals rule the roost in this land?

Will the powers that matter read the proceedings of this case in detail and think of revising the law – and, more importantly, their attitude towards the victims of the crimes?

## 2. Jessica Lall Murder Case (in India)

The trial in Jessica Lall's senseless murder by the power-drunk sons' of politicians should turn into a sacrifice for reform in the archaic criminal justice system of our country. Acquittal of the culprits due to retraction of their earlier statements by the prosecution witnesses has shaken not only the conscience of the nation but even that of the politicians. It is to be noted that such retractions are neither new nor few; and, therefore, for decades, the police officers as well as

Police Reform Commissions have been crying hoarse for reforms in the Criminal Procedure Code and Evidence Act. So far, apparently, the politicians had little reason to 'waste' their 'precious' time on such politically unimportant affairs as protection of the society against depredations by criminals. The public outcry in Jessica Lall's case and our humane President's remarks seem to have woken up our politicians from their slumber.

However, from the present indications and my experience as a police officer, I am not very hopeful of any such amendment being enacted as would be pragmatic, workable and helpful in getting the criminals convicted. The Cr.P.C. was amended in 1973 and all the concerned officers know that the amendments brought out have only further helped the culprits to go scot-free by providing anticipatory bail, independence of prosecutors, etc. No amendment was made to make conviction of the culprits reasonably easy, while ensuring liberty of the innocent. The reason for accused-friendly amendments being enacted is that on legal issues the governments often take advice of only those persons who are or have been defense lawyers. The Law Commission, which is the standing body for recommending amendments, also consists of almost exclusively such persons. Unfortunately, these luminaries have had no experience of investigating criminal cases and the difficulties faced therein, as well as dealing with prosecution witnesses and keeping them firm on their statements during the prolonged course of trial.

To illustrate the above-mentioned point, let us dispassionately consider the workability of a recent recommendation of the Law Commission to rein in witnesses, "it is necessary to amend Section 164 Cr.P.C. to make it mandatory for the investigating officer to get statements of all material witnesses questioned by him during the course of investigation recorded on oath by the magistrate". This recommendation, if accepted, will need manifold increase in the number of investigating officers because then the task of investigator will be not only examination of the witnesses but also of taking them before the magistrate and getting their statements re-recorded. This will also need manifold increase in the number of magistrates, because they will have to find time not only to record the statements on oath during investigation but also to confirm them during trial and face cross-examination by defense lawyers. It is to be considered that even today the police is extremely hard-pressed for time to register and investigate the cases at hand, and, in the courts substantial number of witnesses summoned are returned unexamined daily due to paucity of time, then how will they find time for this additional work. And then, who will stop the witnesses from retracting their statements during trial on the excuse that they had given earlier statement under threat from the magistrate or the court's staff. And this excuse may not always be imaginary, because I remember that in a trap case against a policeman I was summoned as a witness and my statement was recorded in the court room by the court staff while the judge was sitting (or may be sleeping) in his chamber. In such a circumstance, the witness can easily be threatened or misled by any person present in the court room.

If we are serious about the security of the society and justice to the victim of crime, we should adopt simple and workable procedures. Our Cr.P.C. prohibits the investigating officers from getting the statements of witnesses signed by them. This provision should be done away with as it does not exist either in English

Law or in the laws of any civilized democracy. Instead, it should be made mandatory for the I.Os. to get the statements of the witnesses signed by them. Witnesses' signatures will give some sanctity to the statements recorded by the I.O. and may deter the witnesses to some extent from retracting. Further, our Evidence Act provides that the statement recorded by the I.O. can be used during trial only for contradiction and not for corroboration – meaning thereby that it can be used to help the accused and not for strengthening the prosecution. Why should the judge be not given liberty to consider the statements dispassionately and take a fair view on them? Again our Evidence Act prohibits the confessions of the accused persons recorded by or in the presence of police officers from being produced before the court, while in all Western countries confessions made before police officers are not only admissible but are generally the mainstay of the prosecution. In India the police officer has to take the confessing accused to the magistrate who is also not authorized to record the confession immediately, but is duty bound to allow him advice of advocate and give him reasonable time for rethinking before recording his confession. This provision makes confessions by the culprits near impossibility. It is obvious that a culprit is more likely to confess and come out clean at the initial stage when he faces a police officer, rather than later when he gets tutored by an advocate. And since in any case the accused has the liberty to retract his confession during trial, why the confession recorded by a police officer be not admissible as evidence?

Unfortunately, the laws enacted during British Raj were based on distrust of police and there has been a trend of further strengthening the same. During the same period, the British enacted different laws, which were based on trust of the police, for their country. If the aim is to provide justice to victims of crime also while ensuring liberty of the innocent, then strengthening of trustworthiness of both – the prosecution and the defense – will have to be kept in mind while making laws. All knowledgeable persons know that if police officers use dirty tricks to get an accused convicted, the defense counsels use dirtier tricks to get criminals acquitted. Real protection to witnesses lies in conviction of criminals. If after the trial the criminals have the last laugh, no witness protection program will succeed. So, the laws should be amended so that they provide reasonably level playing field to both sides – the prosecution and the defense. Amendments made on suggestions of defense lawyers and judges (who generally rise from the ranks of defense lawyers) only, tend to make investigations and prosecutions more accused-friendly. This is like making Ganges more unclean through Ganges Action Plan.

□

# Transparency in Police

Transparency in the government is the buzzword today. The monarchies and the dictatorships of olden times were not responsible to the people and had no obligation to inform the public about their intentions and activities. With the advent of democracies in which governments are expected to be of the people, by the people and for the people, the demand for transparency in the govt. has grown steadily. The people have been asserting their right to know through their elected representatives as well as individually and the press has been asserting its right to inform the public about entire gamut of governmental activity. Various commissions and committees on administrative reforms have also favored an open govt. The National Police Commission has also recommended that police should be made accountable to the public and subordinated to the Law alone and not to the administrative officers or their political masters. The implementation of this recommendation will itself entail considerable, if not complete, openness in police work. However, the concept of total transparency in police needs closer examination.

Transparency in governmental activity is expected to result in following positive effects in the functioning of the administration:

1. Better appreciation of the performance of the govt. by the public.

2. More adherence to rules by the government servants because of continued public scrutiny.
3. Greater possibility of taking corrective measures before harm to persons or to the nation is done.
4. Less opportunity for corruption or high-handedness in govt. work.

All this will work perfectly in case of such departments of the government whose objectives are to create visible and measurable material gains, but in many a situation impassable difficulties will arise if total transparency is observed in departments that deal with the conduct of human beings. Construction of roads, rails, ships, power houses, dams, etc. and creation of agricultural or industrial wealth and also its distribution are all measurable activities but human proclivity towards crime, his designs for anti-social behavior, his schemes for concealing the guilt and debunking the police and the courts, etc. are not visible and measurable or even easily fathomable. Since human mind is not transparent, observance of total transparency by police in its dealings with human beings may not only be self-defeating but also counterproductive in many cases. Wise parents do not tell the entire truth in their answers to their children's questions, nor do the wise husbands or wives reveal their entire past or entire personality before their spouses. Sociologists confirm that selective concealment of truth helps develop better personalities among children or maintain better inter-personal relations in the family and the society.

Crimes are mostly committed by indulging secretly in anti-social behavior and expert defense against punishment is created by concealing the truth rather than revealing it. Therefore, making it obligatory on police to be totally transparent in its actions against criminals will tantamount to creating uneven playing

(d) Is it really possible to get a criminal convicted without padding the evidence in a society where rarely an actual witness comes forward to give evidence and where defense counsels have no qualms of conscience in producing pure untruth before the courts?

(e) Is it possible to successfully prosecute a terrorist who is feared not only by witnesses but also by the counsels and courts? If not, then will it be possible for the police to curb the activities of a terrorist in a totally transparent environment?

The capture and killing of Osama bin Laden after invading foreign territory is not provided in any statute book, yet considering the futility of any transparent method against the monster, there is a general feeling of action being warranted under the circumstances.

3. *Communal riots and other public disorder situations* – While transparency demands that the public should be promptly informed about the cause and developments related to such disorders but the experience shows that such a disclosure may sometimes aggravate the situation or make the position of police officers untenable.

4. *Intelligence collection* – This may be relating to crime, politics, or anti-national activities. In all cases, this has to be a secret activity. Transparency in intelligence collection will defeat the very purpose for which it is done.

But there can be no justification for any secretiveness for the purpose of illegal gratification, revengeful act, mindless and heartless brutality, or partisan behavior. All efforts are needed to ensure that the need for secretiveness in certain specific circumstances is not made an excuse for illegal or irresponsible acts. There is a commonly used phrase 'good faith' in police, which is considered to be the yardstick for judging the culpability of a non-transparent action by policemen. This can be upgraded as 'good-faith and careful consideration'. Then the necessity of transgressing transparency in police work should be judged on this yardstick.

A society gets the police it deserves. Similarly, a society has to evolve itself to deserve higher degree of transparency in police work.

□

# Politically Inappropriate Talks on Corruption

Thanks to A. Raja, Kalmadi and Anna Hazare. It has now become fashionable not only to talk, but also to form associations, organize demonstrations and sit on *dharnas* against corruption. And an all-powerful Lokpal is considered to be the *Ramban-Oshadhi* against corruption of every form or magnitude. However, in deference to political propriety, rarely a voice is raised against such inappropriate actions of the government as well as its three wings of administration, as have been the most important causes of rising corruption among the government employees. Lokpal might rein in a few high-ups, but he will never be able to intervene in the day-to-day corruption of the horde of corrupt government employees. And government employees are the abettors, perpetrators as well as controllers of corruption.

It is true that today *Netas* control the reins of bureaucracy and to a large extent that of bureaucratic corruption, yet it cannot be gainsaid that initially *Netas* were either too honest, too meek or too ignorant to indulge in brazen corruption like today. It is the bureaucracy – managed and controlled in the field as well as in the secretariat exclusively by the I.A.S./ P.C.S. – that taught the *Netas* the art and science of corruption and gradually fell from the position of advisor to that of a crawling slave. In fact, the I.A.S. – which was the new name for Steel-Frame given to I.C.S. by the British – ensured that democracy never devolved in governmental services. The unitary and arbitrary control of various services by the I.A.S. without commensurate responsibility demoralized other services, and even honest officers of other services had to resort to corrupt practices, if their bosses in the administrative service so demanded.

The service rules of government employees – and particularly those of All India Services – were unduly protective towards the employees; therefore, it has always been a Herculean task to punish an employee. And, unfortunately, the post-independence governments have been making these rules more and more employee-friendly. For example, in the state of U.P. earlier the departmental proceedings against policemen were dealt with under the Indian Police Act, but later this was replaced by Civil Services Act bringing policemen on par with all other employees. Similarly, stringent provisions of P.A.C. Act were also made inapplicable by the new Civil Services Act. Even if some officer took the pains and courage to punish an employee, there is provision for appeal and then revision within the department and, thereafter of course, for fighting legal battle in the courts. And the decision of the punishing authority is usually overturned by one of these authorities. This demoralizes the punishing officers.

The process of demoralizing strict officers was also expedited, although vicariously, by a circumstance rarely discussed in open forums, although often mentioned by senior officers in private talks. Those who have been part of Indian bureaucracy in the early days, know it well that in their zeal to protect the rights of workers – who were presumed to be exploited even if they were the worst exploiters of the liberal system – frequent grant of stay-orders by courts against transfer, suspension and dismissal orders of the erring employees resulted in demoralizing the punishing authority and emboldening the undisciplined and corrupt employees. From my personal experience as a senior officer, I can state with confidence that on many occasions, interference by *Netas* did not demoralize me so much as some of the court orders staying or overturning my orders to punish the subordinates. Nothing can be more humiliating for an honest officer to get his order being thrown back on his face by a corrupt or undisciplined subordinate.

Reservation in promotions proved to be the last straw to break the back of honest officers. It is an eye opener to go through the proceedings of any departmental promotion committee. All the vacancies at higher level to which promotions are to be given are marked as 'general' or 'reserved' according to a roster prescribed by the government. And each promotion has to be made accordingly. Concomitantly, in many vacancies of reserved category such candidates have to be promoted who are not only junior to general candidates but also inefficient, undisciplined, and thoroughly corrupt. Now only a foolishly optimistic person should expect honest behavior from such dishonest employees, who are assured of their promotion on caste-basis. Many a reserved category police constables have been heard telling on the face of their head constables, "*Deewan Ji, chup raho. Tum jo bhi chaho mere khilaf likh do, Sub-inspector to mai hi tumse pahle banunga.*" In such a scenario, only too naïve a person should expect any senior officer to be able to rein in the corrupt subordinate. Since in many states, a new rule has been issued, according to which junior reserved category officials bypass their general category seniors at each stage of promotion, all top posts of every state department are being filled by reserved category officers alone. All senior, honest and hardworking officers of general category have to subserve the junior, inefficient and dishonest officers of the reserved category.

Unfortunately, there are no Anna Hazares to go into the nitty-gritty of these dishonest-friendly policies and sit on *dharna* against them. People either don't know these details or are simply shy of speaking something perceived to be politically inappropriate. The ignorance of administrative details is so widespread that in the panel for Lokpal Bill, no police officer, whose duty is to catch and prosecute a corrupt person, was included while two such members were included whose profession had been to get the corrupt acquitted by the courts. Perhaps this is because it is politically appropriate to include judges, advocates or the I.A.S. officers in any panel on legal matters (refer to the composition of Law Commissions/Human Rights Commissions, etc. of the Centre or the States) and a political blasphemy to include a police officer, although he spends his whole career in facing the nitty-gritty of laws of crime. Some *dalit* leaders have demanded inclusion of a *Dalit* in the panel – and, it does not require great brains to guess which type of legal luminary would be the choice of such leaders for Lokpal.

Nothing substantial can be achieved in attacking corruption, if we do not gather enough courage to speak freely against the causative factors of corruption.

□□□